PIVOT POINT

PIVOT POINT FUNDAMENTALS: COSMETOLOGY

CLIENT-CENTERED DESIGN

ISBN 978-1-940593-43-2

1st Edition
4th Printing, October 2021
Printed in China

Pivot Point International, Inc.
Global Headquarters
8725 West Higgins Road, Suite 700
Chicago, IL 60631 USA

847-866-0500
pivot-point.com

2
32

CONTENTS

104^{c} // CLIENT-CENTERED DESIGN

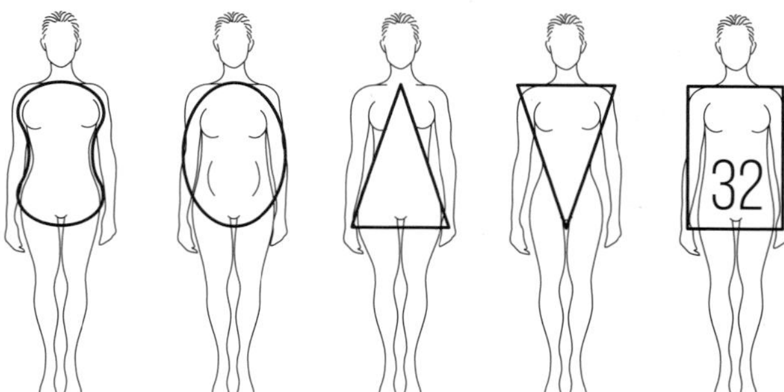

68

75

58

104C.1 DESIGN CONNECTION

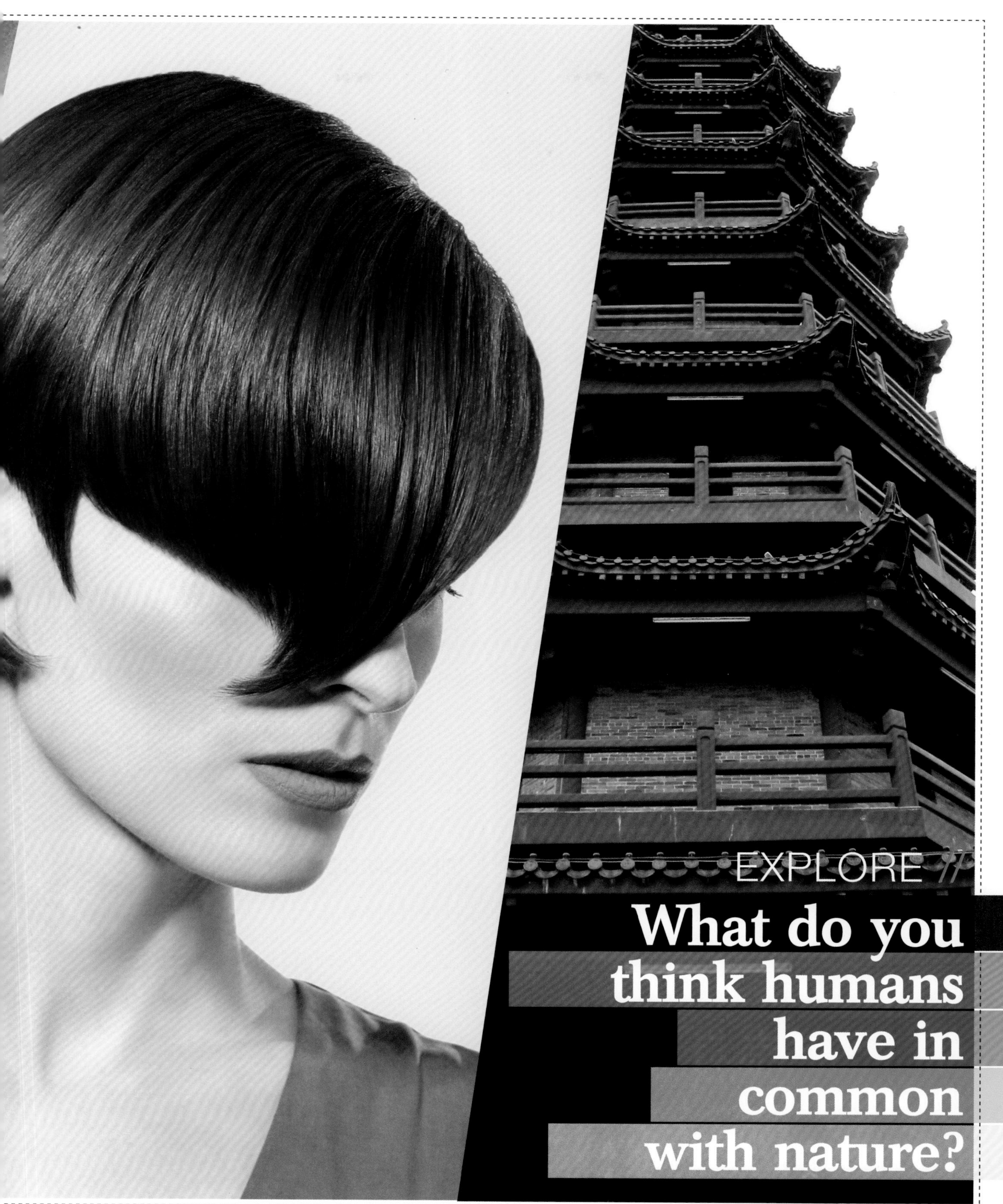
EXPLORE //
What do you think humans have in common with nature?

INSPIRE //

Architecture, paintings, sculpture and hair design—all are composed with forms, textures and colors inspired by nature.

ACHIEVE //

Following this lesson on *Design Connection*, you'll be able to:

- Provide examples of how to see and think as a designer
- Identify the three design elements that comprise every object in the world
- Identify the four design principles related to the design elements
- Provide examples of ways to create as a designer
- Provide examples of ways to adapt as a designer

FOCUS //

DESIGN CONNECTION

See and Think As a Designer

Design Elements

Design Principles

Create As a Designer

Adapt As a Designer

THE FORM OF THE DANCE INSPIRES THE FORM OF THE ARCHITECTURE

104^c.1 | DESIGN CONNECTION

We define **design** as the arrangement of shapes, lines and ornamental effects to create an artistic whole. Design is all around you and impacts your life every day in many ways. The way your furniture is designed affects whether it's pleasing to look at and whether it's functional. The same holds true for fashion, architecture and hair design. You will be arranging your clients' hair in ways that will be both functional and aesthetically pleasing.

Hair design is an art form, like sculpting, painting, architecture and fashion design. Some things designers and artists in these fields have in common:

» Creative compositions are produced on a specific medium–your medium is hair.

» Specialized tools, training and skills are used.

» An understanding of design elements and design principles is needed, as well as a healthy dose of inspiration.

The more open you are to inspiration, the more creative you'll be. And by following a process for becoming a hair designer, you will be well on your way to a successful career.

The design connection process, also referred to as the Four Cornerstones of Design, is all about:

» Seeing as a designer
» Thinking as a designer
» Creating as a designer
» Adapting as a designer

COLOR PATTERNS IN NATURE INSPIRE HAIR COLOR DESIGN

Inspiration can come from nature, art, architecture, music, dance, movies, fashion—anything that you see, hear, taste, smell and touch—or your own **imagination.** You can be inspired by a line, a shape, a texture, a color, a detail or an overall impression.

SEE AND THINK AS A DESIGNER

Training yourself to see and think as a designer will help you form a mental picture of the design you want to create, which includes the big picture as well as the specific details of the design.

Seeing as a designer means observing the world and objects around you and making connections among the different things you see.

Thinking as a designer means analyzing what you see, visualizing a new design and organizing a plan that will enable you to create that design.

By practicing this process, your brain will have more "food for thought" as you make design decisions for your clients, and you'll avoid producing the same designs over and over again.

QUALITATIVE AND QUANTITATIVE ANALYSIS

To strengthen your observational skills:

» Start by learning how to separate the parts from the whole, which is known as qualitative analysis.

» Then, analyze those parts individually, which is known as quantitative analysis.

In qualitative analysis:

» You observe, name and list the parts of an object

» You also list the properties of those parts

Using qualitative analysis, the dress you see here consists of a square neckline and a tight-fitting bodice leading into a full skirt.

In quantitative analysis:

» You begin to determine the amount of each part relative to size, proportion and dimension.

» **Proportion** is defined as any portion or part in relation to the whole.

When you apply quantitative analysis to the same dress, you now see that 1/3 of the dress is a tight-fitting bodice, while 2/3 of the dress is a full skirt.

THREE LEVELS OF OBSERVATION

Many of the things in the world around you, including hair, can take on a variety of appearances, including different shapes, textures, colors and lengths. That's why it's important to have a system for analyzing and talking about what you see. Selective seeing through the three levels of observation gives designers a system for studying, categorizing and communicating the reality around them in a common language.

The **three levels of observation** are:

- Basic
- Detail
- Abstract

BASIC

- Basic observation means you are simply looking at an object and observing its silhouette or its three-dimensional form.
- When viewing a dress, you would see only the outer shape or overall form of the dress, irrespective of any details.
- In this example, the overall shape of the dress is triangular, which is more evident when the dress flares out.

DETAIL

- With a closer, detailed look, you are observing the textures and/or color characteristics, along with any ornamental effects (qualitative analysis).
- Looking at the same dress, you'll register the type of material(s) the dress is made from, such as silk, along with the specific color(s), such as teal and aqua blue.
- With an even closer analysis, you'll notice the pleated detail below the waistline.

ABSTRACT

- With abstract observation, you use the information from the basic and detail levels to view the object in a more conceptual and less literal, concrete way (quantitative analysis).
- You see "a step beyond" the object's face value of how it initially appeared to you.
- In this analysis of the dress, you visualize the pattern that would allow you to re-create the overall shape and its component parts that make up the dress, along with the proportional relationship of one part to another–relative to size, proportion and dimension.

Use qualitative and quantitative analysis as part of the three levels of observation to help you develop your seeing and thinking skills.

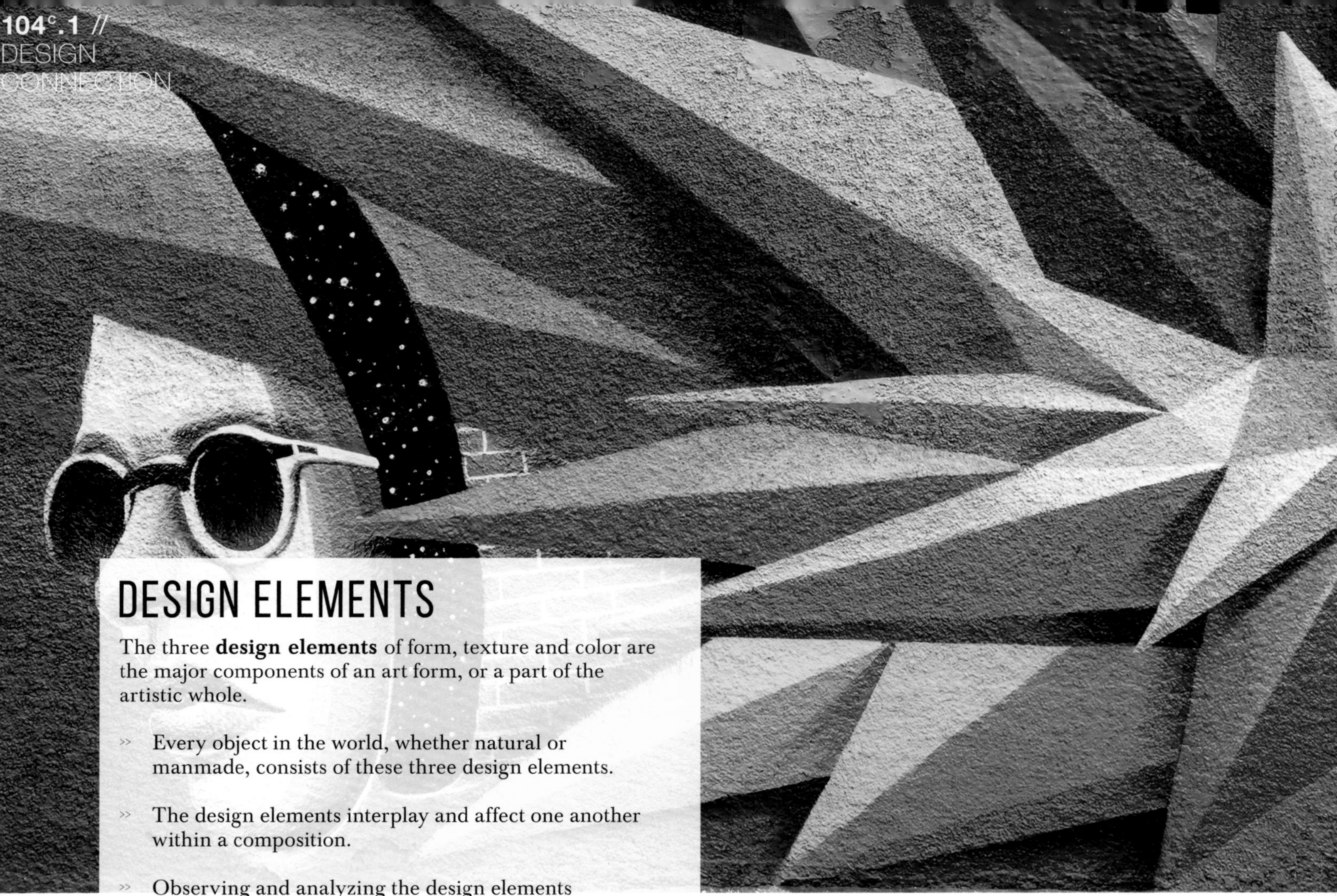

DESIGN ELEMENTS

The three **design elements** of form, texture and color are the major components of an art form, or a part of the artistic whole.

- Every object in the world, whether natural or manmade, consists of these three design elements.
- The design elements interplay and affect one another within a composition.
- Observing and analyzing the design elements individually and together help you understand and create complete designs.
- Viewing a design from all angles enables you to see each of the design elements from different perspectives and how each view relates to the whole.

FORM

Form is the design element that serves as the foundation for every design composition. Once the form is determined, texture and color are added to enhance the form.

In hair design, the terms form and shape are often used interchangeably when describing the outer boundary, outline or silhouette of a design.

- **Form** is the three-dimensional representation of shape; it consists of length, width and depth.
- **Shape** is a two-dimensional representation of form consisting of length and width.
- There are three major categories of forms and shapes:
  - Rectilinear – Consists of horizontal and vertical lines
  - Triangular – Consists primarily of diagonal lines
  - Curvilinear – Consists of curved lines

Geometric Forms and Shapes

THREE-DIMENSIONAL (3D)

RectilinearTriangular

Curvilinear

TWO-DIMENSIONAL (2D)

Square

4 equal sides

Triangle

3 equal sides

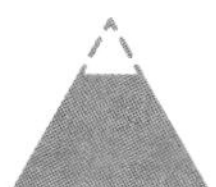

Trapezoid

2 unequal parallel sides

2 equal, nonparallel sides

Circle

Closed, curved shape

Equal radii

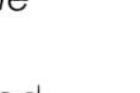

Half-Circle *Crescent*

Derivatives of circle

Rectangle

2 sets of parallel sides

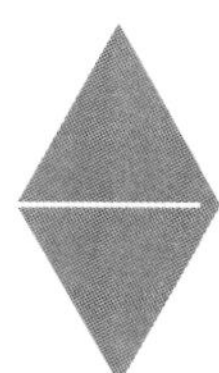

Diamond

2 equal back-to-back triangles

Kite

2 unequal back-to-back triangles

Oval

Closed, curved shape

Unequal radii

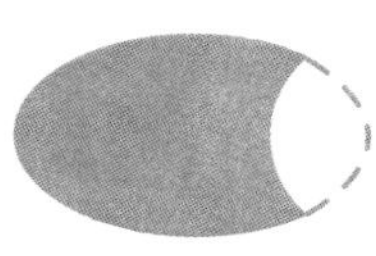

Oblong

Elongated curvature shape with a closed and open end

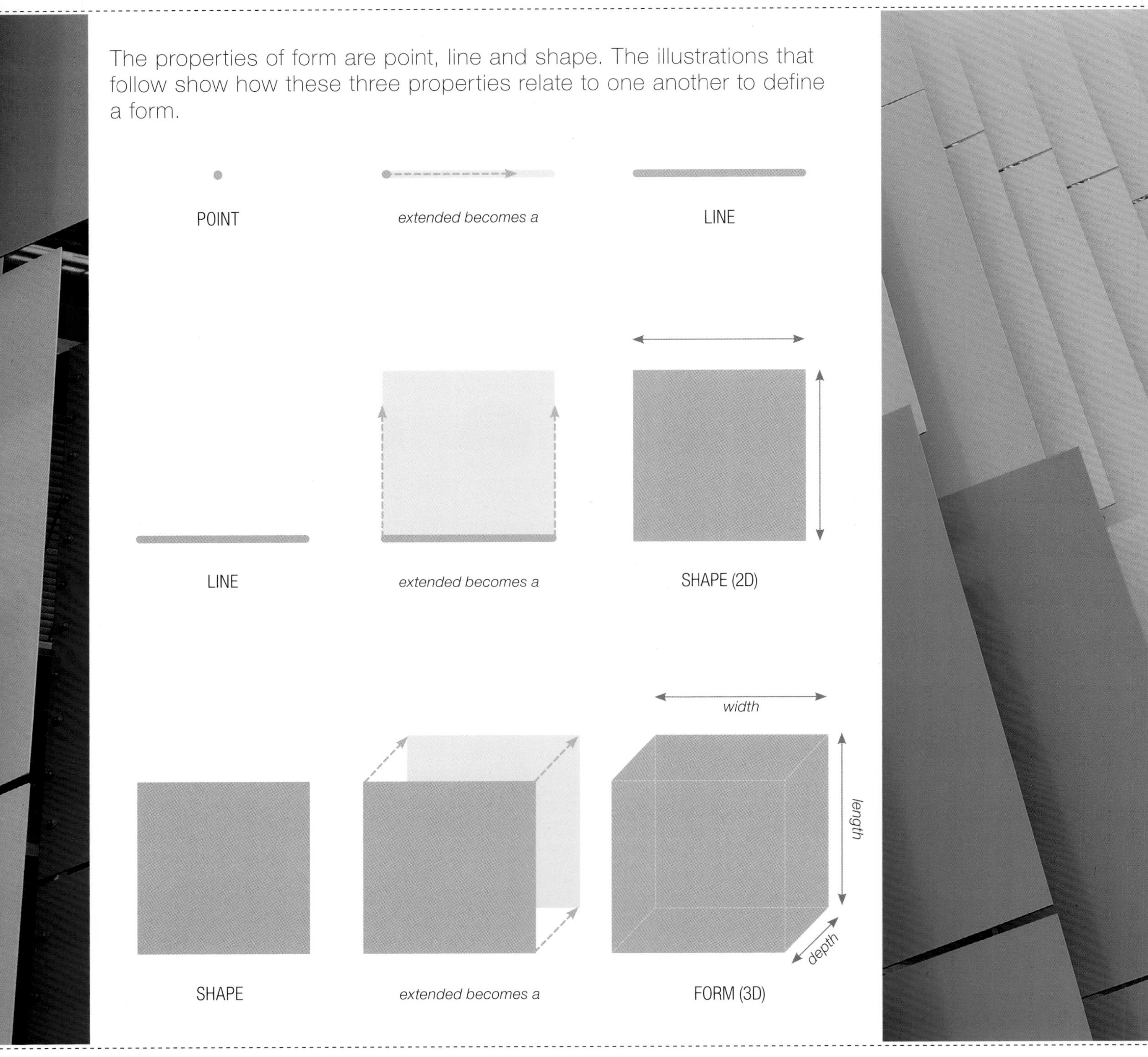
The properties of form are point, line and shape. The illustrations that follow show how these three properties relate to one another to define a form.
POINT
extended becomes a
LINE
LINE
extended becomes a
SHAPE (2D)
width
length
depth
SHAPE
extended becomes a
FORM (3D)

Line

Analysis of form begins with an understanding of its most basic component, the point.

- A **point** is a mark which, when set into motion, becomes a line.
- A **line** is a series of connected points.

The path or direction of a given line can be straight, curved or any combination. Different types of lines can trigger different emotional responses depending on their characteristics. The characteristics of a line can range from thin and delicate to thick and bold. Lines can express strength, delicacy or boldness.

Lines direct your eyes from one point to another. Used properly, lines can produce continuity and unity within a design.

The three straight lines are:

- **Horizontal** – Parallel to the horizon or floor; gives the impression of stability, weight and calmness
- **Vertical** – Perpendicular to the horizon or floor; implies strength, weightlessness and equilibrium
- **Diagonal** – Fall between horizontal and vertical lines; energetic and implies motion

Curved lines can be represented by any of the three straight lines. Curved lines include concave and convex lines.

- Concave lines curve inward, like the inside of a sphere.
- Convex lines curve outward, like the outside of a sphere.

The path of a curved line can be slow and passive or fast and energetic. Curved lines imply softness and can lead your eye fluidly and rhythmically throughout a composition.

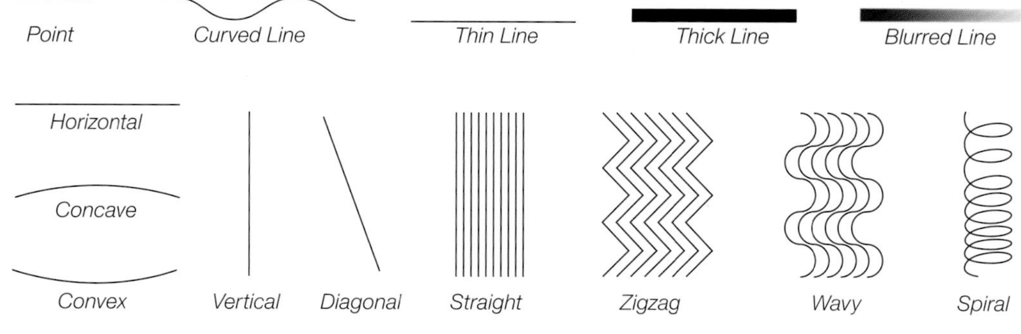

Shape

Shape is a two-dimensional representation of form consisting of length and width but not depth. A shape is generally seen as a flat space, or plane, enclosed by a line that has turned to meet itself. A shape consists of angles and, when extended into space, a shape becomes a form.

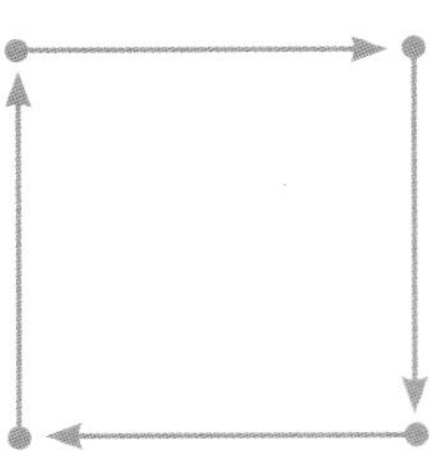

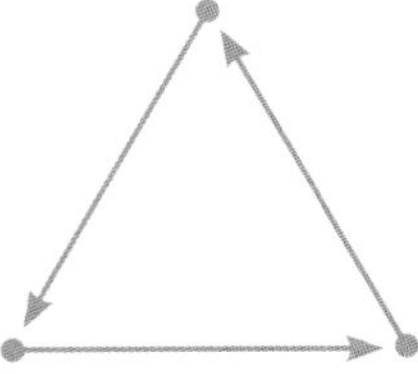

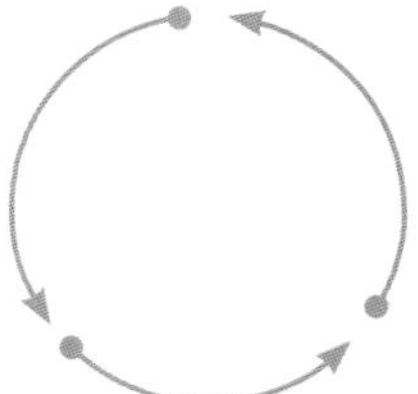

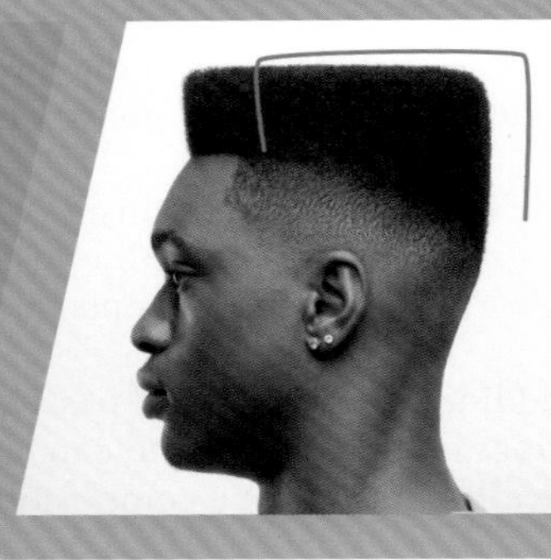

The **celestial axis** is a symbol that will help you identify straight and curved lines, angles and directions. When observing lines in a hair design, note the outer boundary of the form (form line), the direction of the overall form and the lines within the form.

Observing Forms: Nature, Manmade and Hair

Nature creates an unlimited number of forms based on three basic characteristics: rectilinear, triangular and curvilinear. People have interpreted these forms and, through their imagination, developed new forms. Studying forms and shapes that are manmade and found in nature will help you create inspirational new three-dimensional forms in hair.

Bottom row, middle: Tony 7, morguefile

TEXTURE

Texture is the visual appearance or feel of a surface, and it's the design element that creates interest within a design. Surface textures are divided into two main categories:

- Unactivated (smooth)
- Activated (rough/broken)

Observing Textures: Nature, Manmade and Hair

Nature provides a myriad of textures, from soft, smooth surfaces to rough, edgy patterns. Fabrics are rich in textural qualities—from smooth silks to soft cashmeres, to coarse, scratchy woolens. Observing and feeling textures in the world around you will strengthen your observational skills and sense of touch. This in turn will provide you with inspiration from which to draw upon when creating textures in hair.

In hair design, textures can also take on individual qualities of a line such as straight, zigzag and curved.

COLOR

Color is the visual perception of the reflection of light. The design element of color can add depth, dimension and the illusion of texture to a form. All colors are created by a combination of three primary colors:

- Yellow
- Red
- Blue

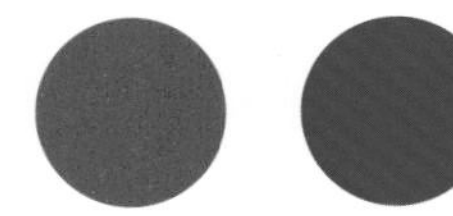

The primary colors are referred to as "pure" colors because they cannot be created by mixing any other colors.

When combining two primary colors together in varying proportions, secondary colors are created:

- Green
- Orange
- Violet

Y = Yellow
R = Red
B = Blue
G = Green
O = Orange
V = Violet

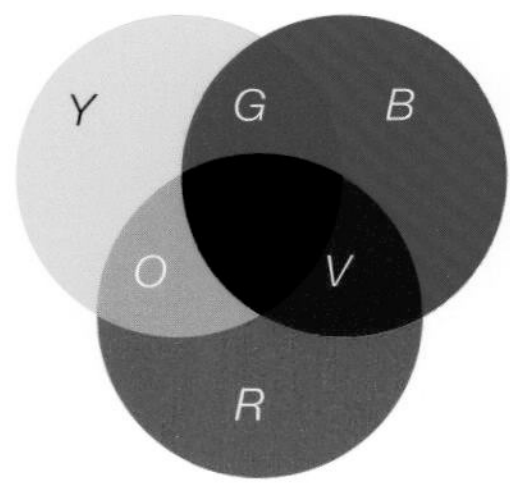

Every color can be categorized into one of three categories: warm, cool or neutral.

- Colors that contain yellow, red or orange are referred to as warm.
- Colors that contain blue, green or violet are referred to as cool.
- Colors that are not predominately warm or cool are referred to as neutral; sometimes called "earth tones," these colors can include various shades of brown, beige and gray.

Observing Colors: Nature, Manmade and Hair

Color and color patterns in nature are limitless and can provide inspirational ideas for hair designs. Colors also communicate emotions, which you can use to personalize the hair designs you create.

- Warm colors like reds, oranges and golds give hair designs a passionate, energetic or exciting feel.
- Cool colors like blues, violets and greens can communicate a strong, edgy or confident quality.
- Using predominately neutral colors can give your clients a flexible canvas that is adaptable to many hair design options.

When creating hair color designs, you can reproduce the colors you see in nature in literal or symbolic ways to capture the essence of what you see.

	NATURE	MANMADE	HAIR
WARM			
COOL			
NEUTRAL			

DESIGN PRINCIPLES

Design principles are the artistic arrangement patterns for the design elements of form, texture and color to follow. The four design principles are:

- Repetition
- Alternation
- Progression
- Contrast

Understanding these four design principles allows you to analyze a composition so you can re-create and adapt designs according to individual preferences. The following are examples of the design principles as they apply to form, texture and color.

REPETITION

With **repetition**, all units are identical except for position. Think of a classic pearl necklace. Repetition can be created throughout a composition or within a specific area. In hair design, repetition creates a feeling of uniformity.

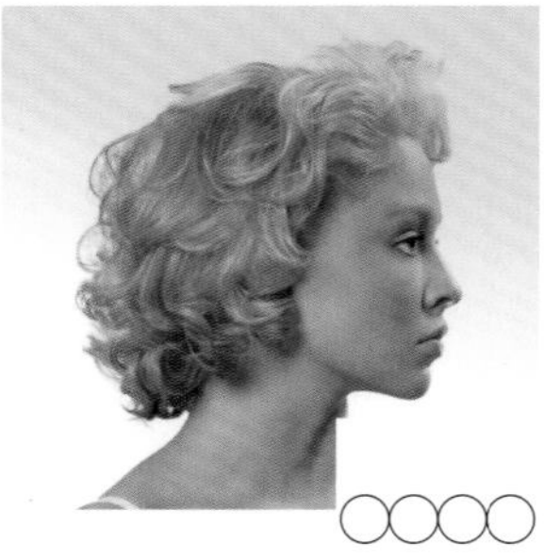

Repetition of Form

Repetition of Texture

Repetition of Color

ALTERNATION

Alternation is a sequential repetition in which two or more units occur in a repeating pattern. Think of the colors on a checkerboard. In hair design, alternation can break up the surface of an object, creating interest.

Alternation of Form

Alternation of Texture

Alternation of Color

PROGRESSION

With **progression**, all units are similar, yet gradually change proportionately in an ascending (increasing) or descending (decreasing) scale. Think of the notes in a musical scale. In hair design, progression can lead the eye rhythmically within a design or draw attention to a point of interest.

Progression of Form

Progression of Texture

Progression of Color

CONTRAST

Contrast is a desirable relationship of opposites. Think of the look of a black tuxedo with a starched white shirt. Contrast creates variety and stimulates interest within a design.

Contrast of Form

Contrast of Texture

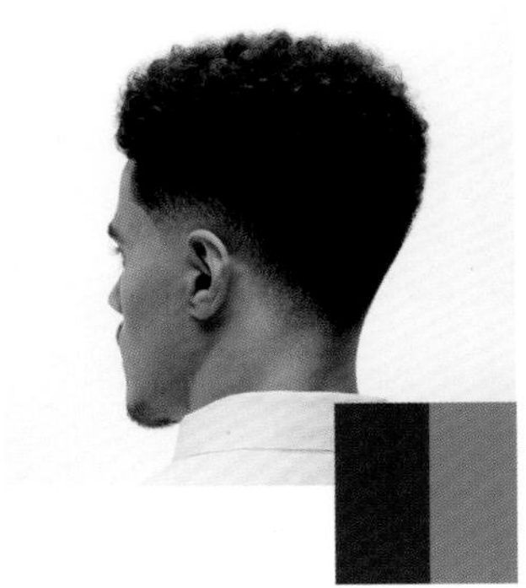

Contrast of Color

BALANCE

Balance is an important part of any design composition. **Balance** is the state of equilibrium existing between contrasting, opposite or interacting elements. When a design is in balance, the arrangement of elements and the proportions within the design are harmonious and pleasing.

There are two types of balance:

Symmetrical balance, or harmonious arrangement

- Created when weight is positioned equally on both sides of a center axis, creating a mirror image
- Focus remains on the silhouette of the design

Asymmetrical balance, or off-center arrangement

- Created when weight is positioned unequally from a center axis
- Visual balance can still be achieved even though the actual mass of the hair is off-center
- Creates a sense of movement and drama and should be personalized to the client
- Extreme asymmetry generally results in a design losing its balance

In other words...

Seeing as a designer is all about:

- Observing the world around you for inspiration
- Connecting what you see to design elements and design principles

Thinking as a designer is all about:

- Analyzing what you see
- Visualizing a new design
- Organizing a plan

SALON**CONNECTION**

Master of Your Craft!

One day, you will apply all your personal creativity, knowledge and skills in the salon. Whether you decide to become a master of one area of hair design, such as cut or color, or you decide to practice all areas of hairdressing, understanding how form, texture and color interrelate will lead you to a successful career. Communication will be critical, not only between you and your client, but also between you and another specialist in the salon in order to share design composition ideas that meet your client's needs.

CREATE AS A DESIGNER

Creating as a designer means:

- Practicing all aspects of hair design to build your expertise
- Performing hair design procedures with focus and precision to produce predictable results

CREATING FORM

In hair, forms are created through sculpting techniques, as well as hair design techniques and long hair design techniques.

SCULPTURE DESIGN

HAIR DESIGN

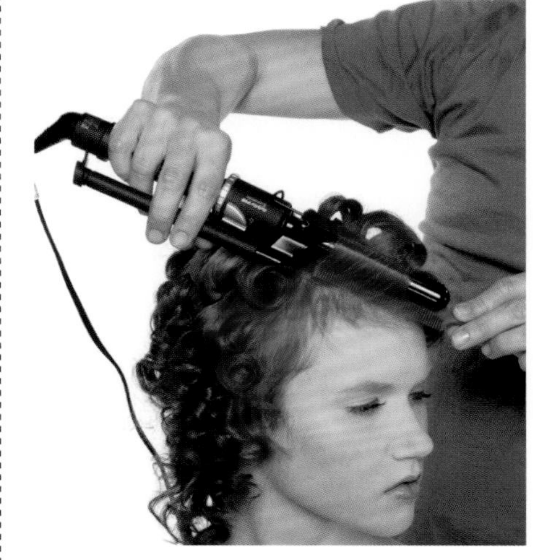

LONG HAIR DESIGN

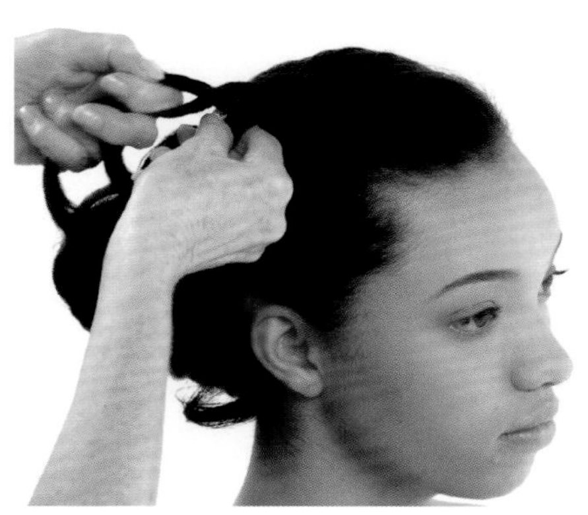

CREATING TEXTURE

Texture patterns can be created through hair design and perming techniques and reduced through chemical relaxing techniques. Sculpting techniques can add texture variables.

HAIR DESIGN

PERM DESIGN

RELAXER DESIGN

CREATING COLOR

Color can be added to hair through the use of hair color products or hairpieces. Color can lead your eye through a design or it can draw the eye to one particular point of interest. Color can also break up the surface appearance of the hair to create the illusion of texture.

HAIR COLOR PIECES

COLOR DESIGN

ADAPT AS A DESIGNER

Adapting is the highest level of design proficiency. Adapting as a designer means that you are able to compose innovative and artistic hair designs by drawing upon your knowledge, skill and vision.

Adapting challenges you to expand your ability to envision and create looks that are appropriate and flattering to each client. The two main components for adapting hair designs are:

- Composing – Integrating knowledge, skill and vision to create a specific hair design
- Personalizing – Ensuring the color, texture, sculpture and overall hair design all meet your clients' individual needs

ADAPT: FORM

Shape on shape creates a focal point at the cheeks.

ADAPT: TEXTURE

Wavy texture expands the form and creates an airy effect.

ADAPT: COLOR

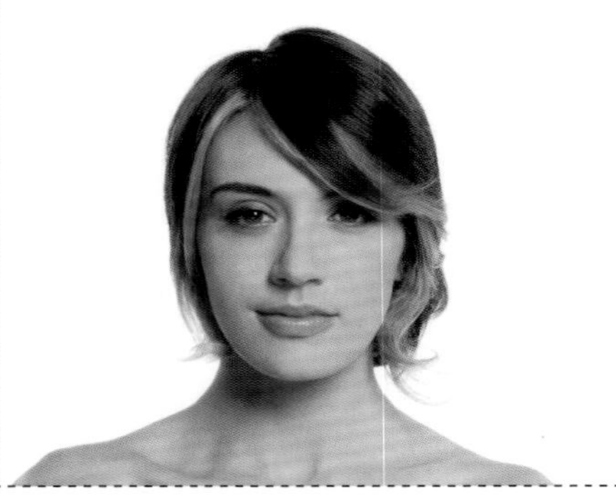

Warmer reddish tones enhance client's skin complexion.

DISCOVER**MORE**

Did you know that nature's creatures are master architects? They personalize and compose designs to include forms, textures and color, just like humans. For example, the male satin bowerbird builds his unique "bower" on the ground to attract a mate. The bower is composed of a trellis-like structure; various colorful blue, yellow and shiny objects; a medley of berries, flowers, even fountain pens and other plastic objects—all used to entice and impress the female. The idea behind the bower structure is to have the female bowerbird stand on one end, peer down through the trellis, and if impressed by what she sees on the other end, she'll walk through the trellis to the other side. If she does that, the male has succeeded with his "design." The bowerbird has violet-blue eyes, and his feathers reflect a deep shiny blue appearance. As the males mature, they include more blue-colored objects in their bower. Some wonder if it's because he thinks being blue himself, blue just might be the most beautiful color. Search the Internet for more of nature's "blue" creatures such as the blue penguin, blue dragon fish and the blue glowing coconut octopus and start composing your unique designs!

The levels of observation, design elements and design principles provide the foundation for creating professional hair designs. Mastering the process of **seeing**, **thinking**, **creating** and **adapting** as a designer will set you apart from the average stylist in the salon.

LESSONS LEARNED

- Seeing as a designer means observing the world and objects around you and making connections using design elements and design principles.
- Thinking as a designer means analyzing what you see, visualizing a new design, and organizing a plan that will enable you to create that design.
- The three design elements are:
  - Form – Three dimensional representation of shape, includes length, width and depth
  - Texture – Visual appearance or feel of a surface; unactivated (smooth), activated (rough/broken)
  - Color – Visual perception of the reflection of light
- The four design principles are:
  - Repetition – All units are identical except for their position
  - Alternation – A sequential repetition in which two or more units occur in a repeating pattern
  - Progression – All units are similar but gradually change proportionately in an ascending or descending scale
  - Contrast – A desirable relationship of opposites
- Creating as a designer means practicing all aspects of hair design to build your expertise and to perform them with focus and precision to produce predictable results.
- Adapting as a designer means composing and personalizing hair designs to meet your client's individual needs.

104^{C}.2
CLIENT CONSIDERATIONS

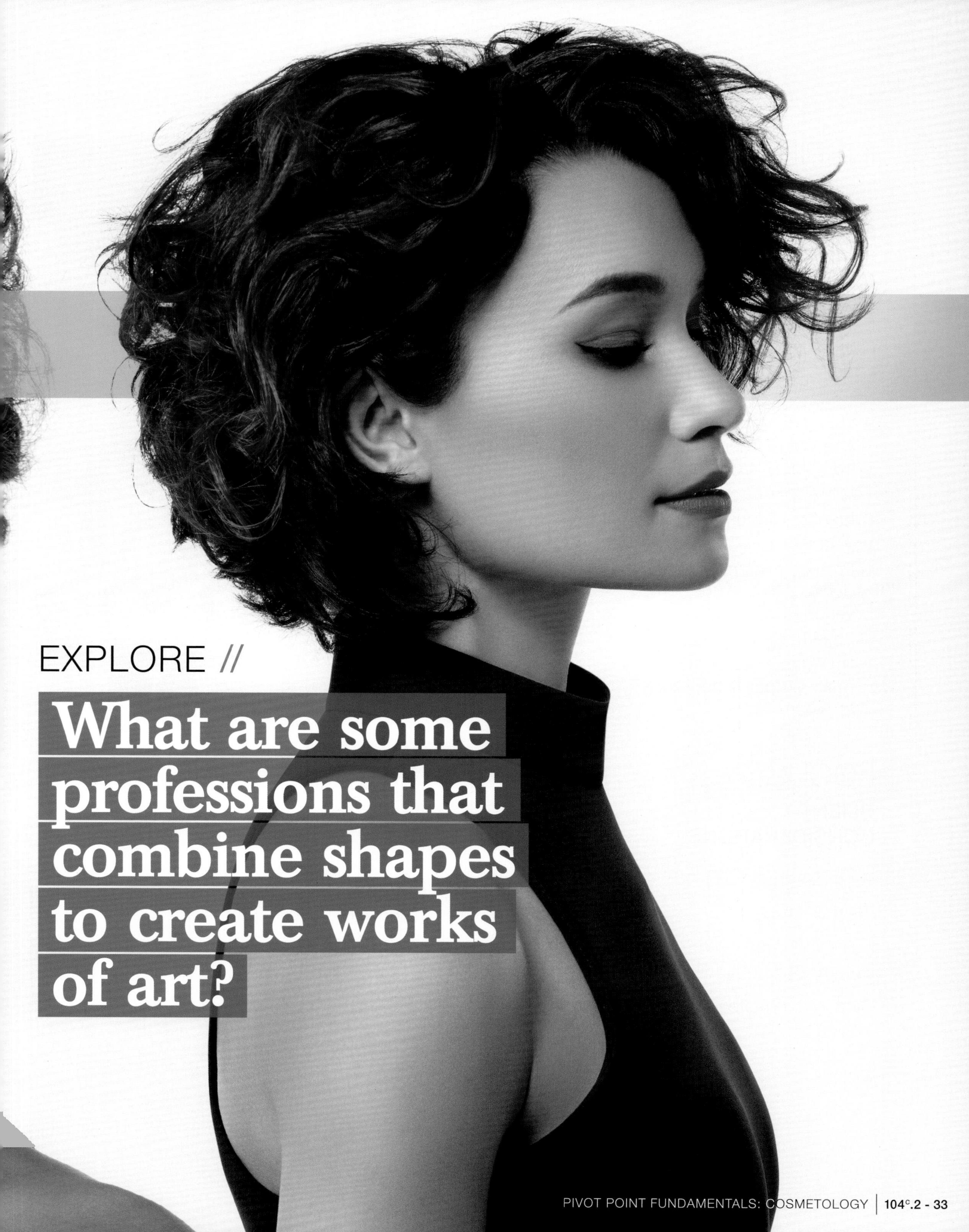

EXPLORE //

What are some professions that combine shapes to create works of art?

INSPIRE //

Learning how to adapt lines and shapes will help you personalize designs for each and every client.

ACHIEVE //

Following this lesson on *Client Considerations*, you'll be able to:

- Describe how hair designs can be adapted to complement different body types
- Identify various body shapes
- Provide examples of hair designs to complement various face shapes
- Identify clothing and lifestyles to consider when making design decisions for your clients

FOCUS //

CLIENT CONSIDERATIONS

Body Types and Shapes

Face Shapes

Hair Color and Natural Coloring

Clothing and Lifestyles

104°.2 | CLIENT CONSIDERATIONS

As a designer, you have the ability to help clients look and feel their best by offering sound design decisions and adapting your knowledge of design composition to each client's particular needs.

To provide your client with the best look:

- Flatter their unique physical features
- Meet the needs of the way they live their daily lives

This requires careful analysis and an understanding of the client's body and facial shape.

How is it possible that a hair design can complement one client's facial features, but not another's? The answer lies in the concept of proportion. The Greek philosopher Plato described beauty as existing in the proportion of things.

Today's expert thinking confirms that proportion plays a major role in people's perception of beauty. As a hair designer, you have the ability to enhance your client's attractiveness by creating a more proportionate harmony between the hair design and the client's face, and between the client's head and body.

The following are suggestions for creating ideal proportions–not hard rules. As a designer, it's important to be aware of the effects your design decisions can have on how a client's body proportions are perceived.

BODY TYPES AND SHAPES

By becoming familiar with body types and shapes, a hair designer can gain insight on making recommendations for personalized hair designs for their clients.

STANDARD PROPORTION BETWEEN HEAD AND BODY

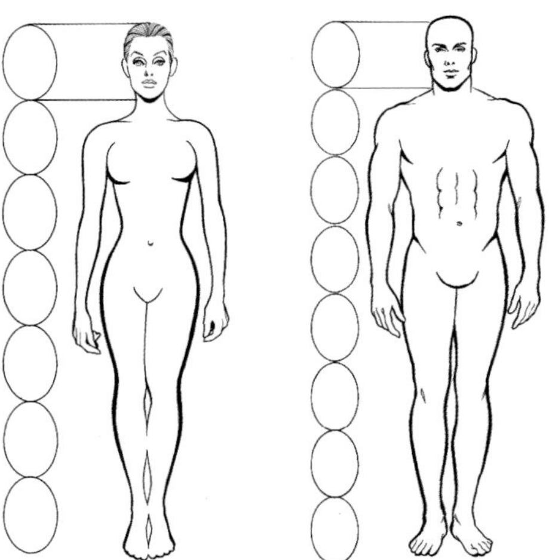

According to the standard proportion most artists use:

- The head of a woman is 1/7 of her overall body height
- The head of a man is 1/8 of his overall body height
- Designs too large or too small for the client's stature will negatively affect ideal proportions between the head and body

BODY TYPES

The variety of human **body types** fall into three main categories:

- Ectomorph
- Mesomorph
- Endomorph

DISCOVER**MORE**

As artists throughout history sketched, painted and sculpted the human body, they discovered some golden rules about the ideal proportions between the body and the head, including the hair. Today those proportions have become a standard that is taught in art classes all over the world. When you incorporate these standards into your work as a hair designer, you will increase your ability to make the best design decisions for your clients. Plato once said, "The good, of course, is always beautiful, and the beautiful never lacks proportion." To see what he meant by this, search the Internet for the "Golden Ratio" as found in nature, art, sculpture and architecture.

Being aware of your client's body type will help you make hair design recommendations that complement them. Determine your client's body type at the beginning of the service by having them stand in front of the mirror so you can see the overall body height and proportions. The following chart identifies the characteristics of the three body types. Keep in mind that not everyone falls into a single category, and most of us have characteristics of two, or even three of the body types.

	ECTOMORPH	MESOMORPH	ENDOMORPH
DESCRIPTION	» **Tall and lanky** » Narrow frame	» **Rectangle-shaped** » Athletic and muscular	» **Short and sturdy** » Soft and round
SHOULDERS/HIPS	Neither are dominant	Dominant shoulders; average hips	Both are wide
LEGS/ARMS/NECK	Long	Balanced proportion	Short
WOMEN (HEIGHT)	5'10" (1.7 m) or taller 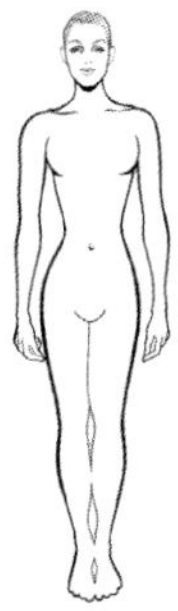	5'5" (1.6 m) - 5'9" (1.7 m) 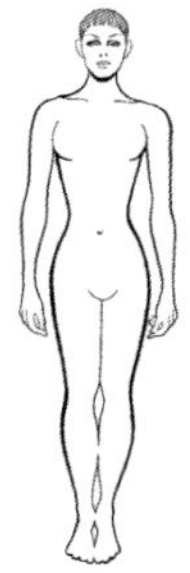	5'4" (1.6 m) or shorter 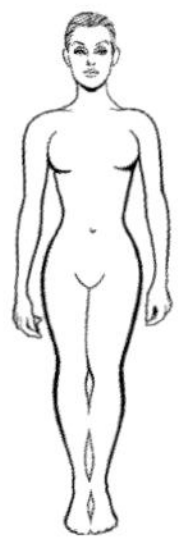
MEN (HEIGHT)	6'1" (1.8 m) or taller 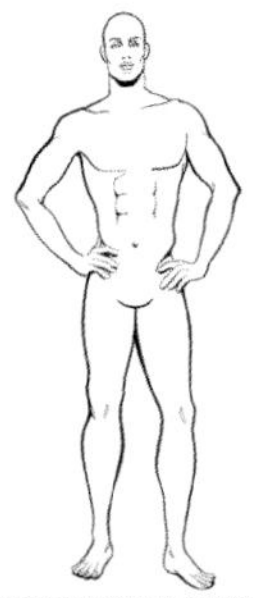	5'7" (1.7 m) - 6'1" (1.8 m) 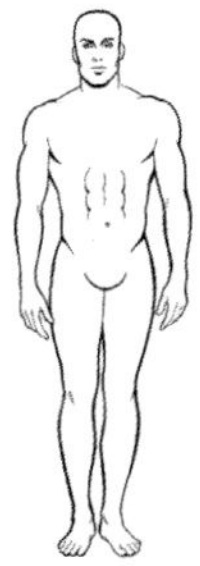	5'7" (1.7 m) or shorter 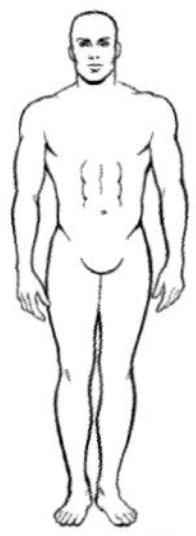
HAIR DESIGN RECOMMENDATIONS	Add volume and/or length to make head appear larger and in better proportion to the rest of the body.	Almost any hair length and hair design is flattering.	Add height and volume on top to balance out proportions.
SHORT VERSUS LONGER LENGTHS	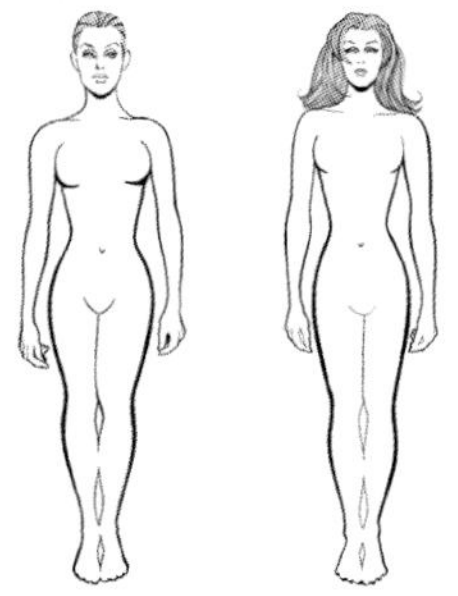	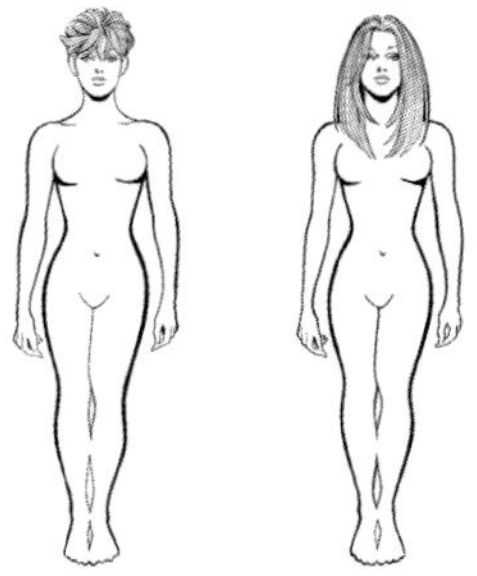	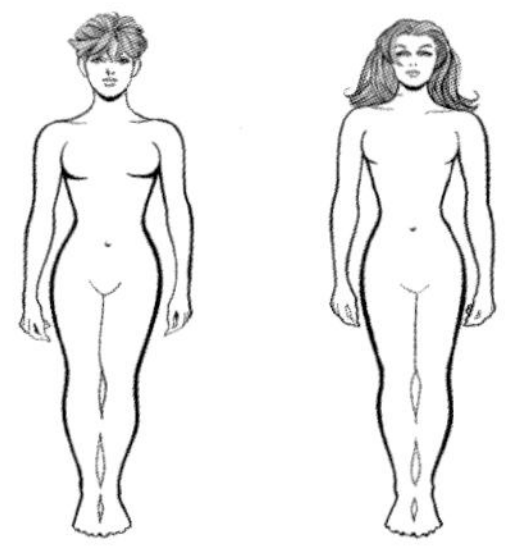
SHORT VERSUS LONGER LENGTHS (MEN)	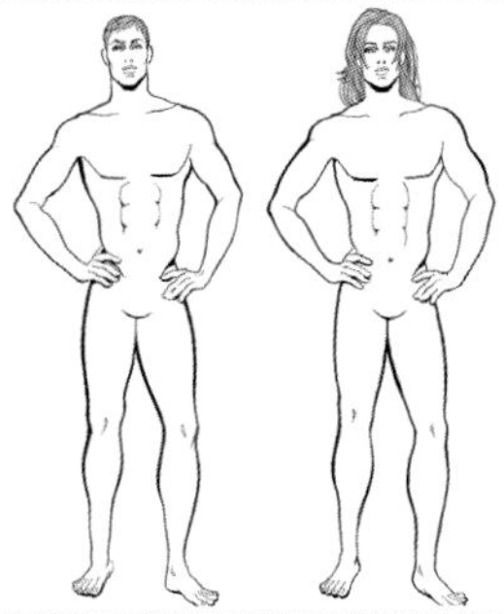	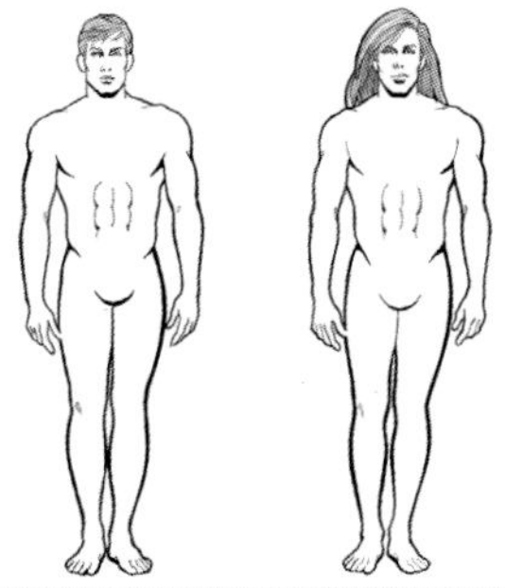	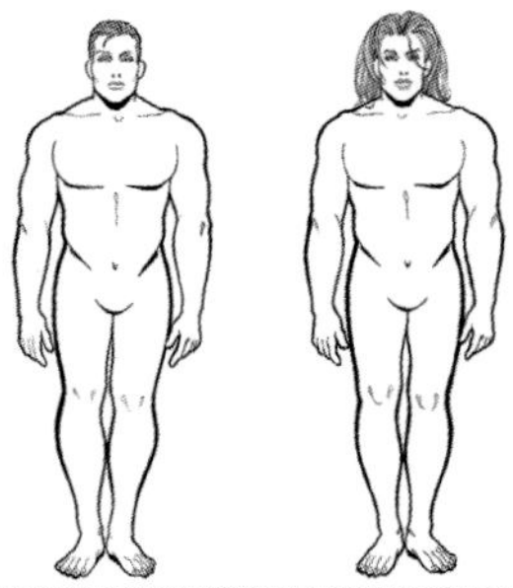

BODY SHAPES

The overall body type, or build, can be further analyzed according to body shape.

General body shapes include:

- Hourglass
- Apple
- Triangle (pear)
- Inverted triangle
- Rectangle

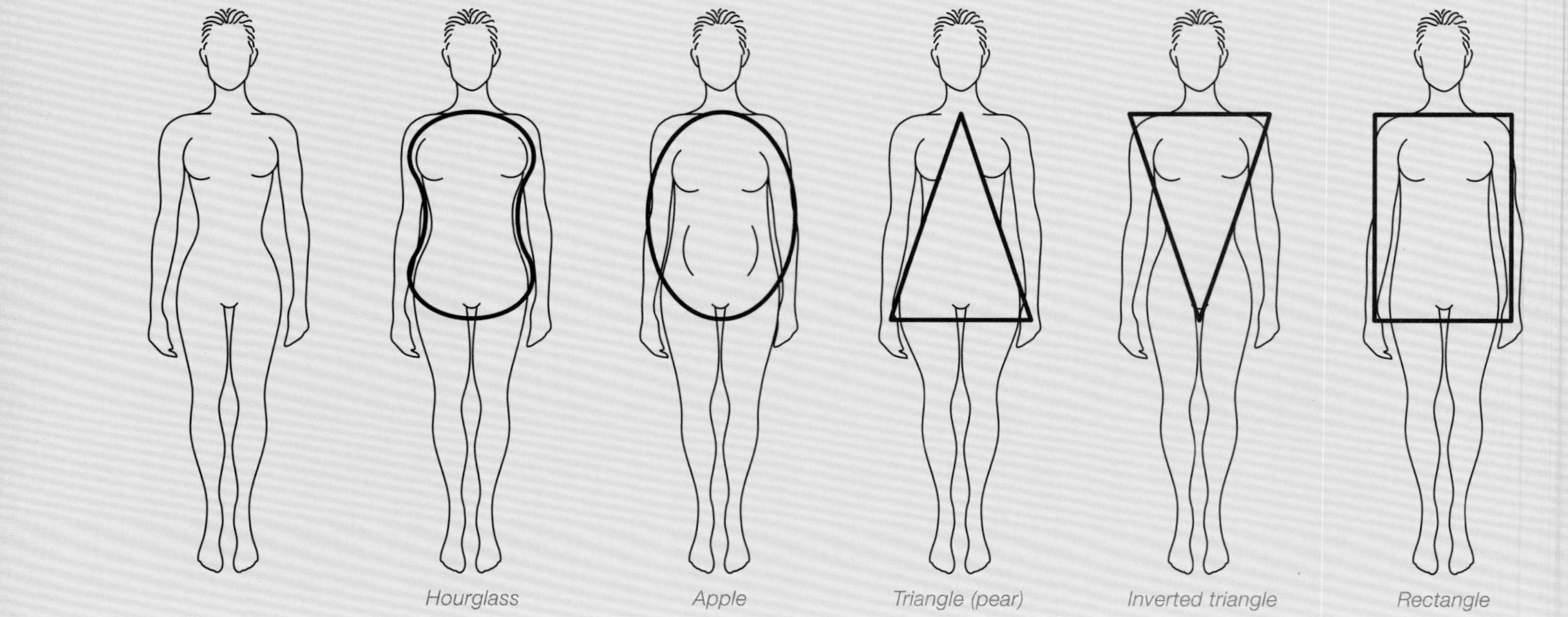

When considering the body shape:

- Identify widest area of body
- Visualize client's overall body silhouette
- Imagine amount of volume needed to bring widest area into proportion with rest of body
- Add darker colors to diminish wider areas

The following is a list of recommendations for each body shape:

SHAPES	DESCRIPTION	
HOURGLASS	Rounded bottom and thighs; small waist, full bust	
	Do: Wear clothes fitted at waist Wear fabrics that drape smoothly	**Don't:** Wear oversized clothes Emphasize the fullest areas
APPLE	Rounded shoulder line; average to big bust; fullness around the middle	
	Do: Wear cowl necklines Wear tailored clothing with soft drape styles	**Don't:** Wear clothing that is wide at the waist Wear cropped tops
TRIANGLE (PEAR)	Full hips; defined waist; shoulders more narrow than hips; small top half	
	Do: Wear dark colors to diminish the widest area Add bright colors and prints on top	**Don't:** Wear oversized tops Emphasize the widest area
INVERTED TRIANGLE	Bottom half smaller than top; straight and squared shoulder line	
	Do: Wear darker colors on top to diminish width Wear V-necklines	**Don't:** Accentuate shoulders with wide lapels or collars Puffy sleeves
RECTANGLE	Narrow shoulders; small bust; non-defined waist; narrow hips	
	Do: Add feminine details Wear fitted tops	**Don't:** Wear male-structured clothing Baggy tops

As mentioned earlier, there are no hard rules. As a designer, it's up to you to make recommendations to your client, but ultimately it's their decision whether or not they agree with your recommendations. For example, a large figure could be enhanced with more hair—a design that is too small in proportion will make the body look even larger. While a small figure could be enhanced with less hair—for a short, small-boned figure, a design that is too large will make the body appear even smaller. In some cases, the existing hair length might not be long enough to carry out a chosen design immediately. It might be necessary to let some areas of the hair grow.

Large Figure – More Hair

Better Balance

Small Figure – Less Hair

Better Balance

BODY FEATURES

Besides the overall height and body proportion, there are also individual body features that, if dominant, need to be considered separately. The two main body features needing particular consideration are the neck and shoulders.

Neck

Although the length of the neck often corresponds to a client's overall body shape, the neck should also be considered on its own when making design decisions.

SHORT NECK
Keep hair close or off of face

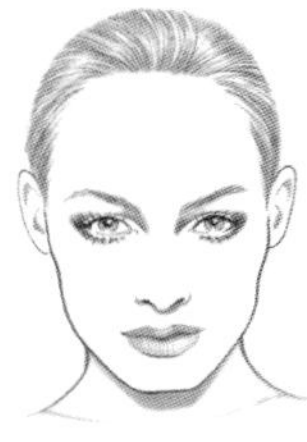

- Avoid volume at neck area, as it accentuates shortness of the neck
- Long, wispy lengths visually elongate
- Outlining around neckline should be narrow and elongated

LONG NECK
Frame with hair

- Surround neck with mass and fullness
- Try longer, fuller hair at perimeter
- Shorter designs should still show hair along neck from front view
- Leave nape area longer and fuller
- Sculpt a horizontal design line at bottom to imply weight or fullness

Shoulders

In most cases the shoulders reflect the overall body shape. A tall and lanky client will often have narrow shoulders, while a short and sturdy client will have wide shoulders. Analyze each client's individual shoulder shape and make your design decisions accordingly.

WIDE SHOULDERS
Add elongation

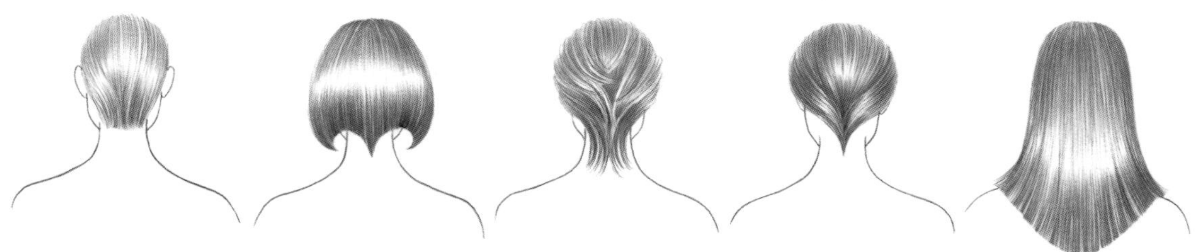

- Wide shoulders can benefit from a hair design with a narrowing design line in back.
- The design lines could be any lines that imply a narrow or a steep V-shape. These lines give the illusion of narrowing the shoulders and stretching the back.

NARROW SHOULDERS
Add width

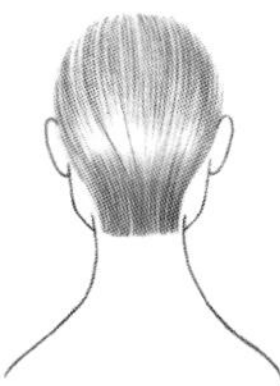
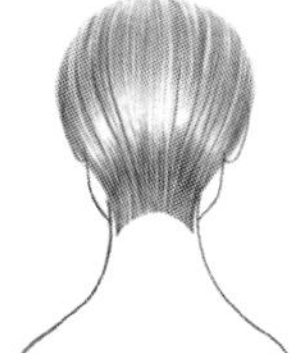

- Narrow shoulders can benefit from a hair design with added width in the back.
- The design lines could imply horizontal lines or an A-shape. Flat and wide, oval lines also work well.
- All lines need to be sculpted at low angles to add fullness and weight.

FACE SHAPES

Facial structure often reflects body structure. Many tall and lanky clients have elongated faces, while short clients often have wide faces. The right hair design can frame and make any face beautiful.

To determine the most appropriate design, analyze the face using criteria such as:

- Bone structure
- Hairline
- Widest areas
- Most dominant areas

Use the following questions as a guide to help you easily and clearly determine which facial shape is present:

- Is the face long and narrow, or short and wide?
- Is the shape of the face angular or rounded?
- Which area of the face is most dominant?

THREE-SECTIONING

Three-sectioning is an effective way to measure the proportions of the face. It's done by measuring the three sections of the face:

1. Front hairline to the middle of the eyebrows
2. Middle of the eyebrows to the tip of the nose
3. Tip of the nose to the tip of the chin

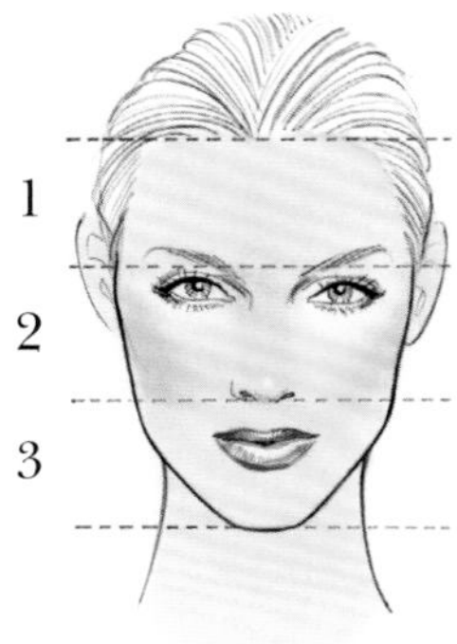

These sections are considered harmoniously proportioned if they are of equal length:

- More than ½" (1.25 cm) difference between any of these sections is not considered harmonious
- Hair designs and makeup can be used to create the illusion of balance

To measure the face using the three-sectioning technique:

- Comb and pin all hair off the face
- Place client in front of a mirror
- Remove client's glasses and jewelry
- Measure three sections with a tape measure or sculpting comb

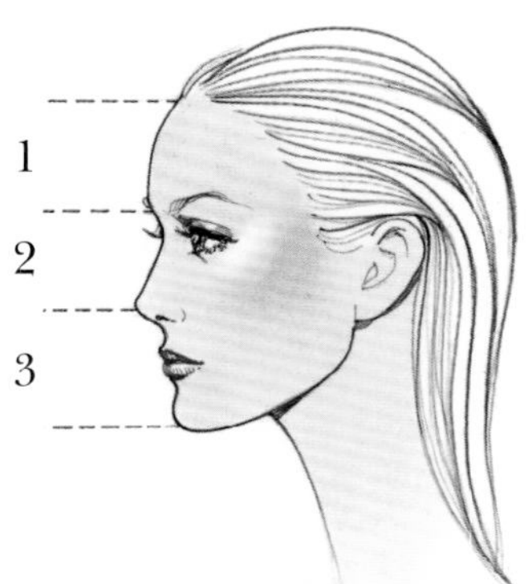

Having the client observe in the mirror while you are three-sectioning will help the client understand the reasons behind the design decisions you will be recommending.

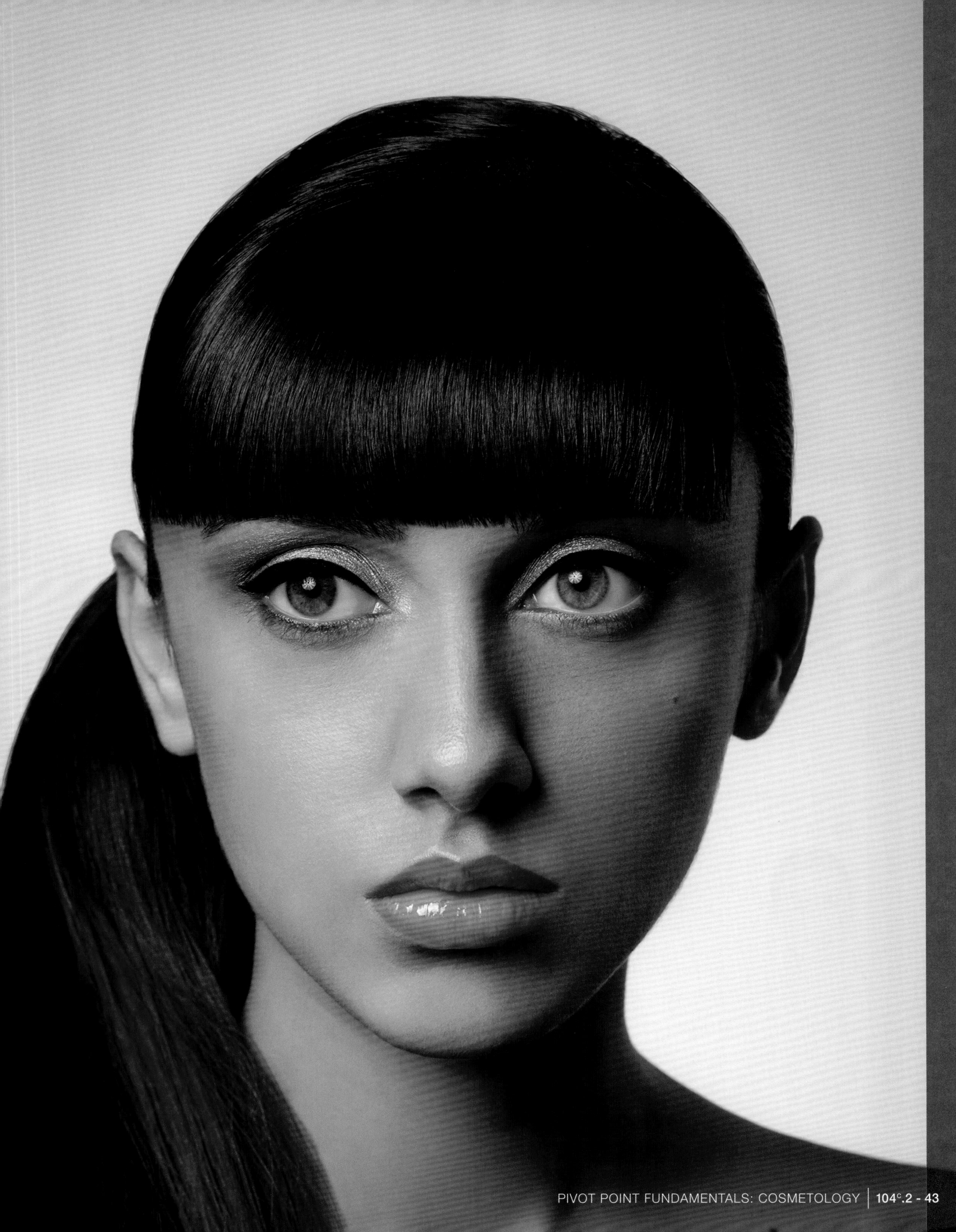

COMMON FACE SHAPES

There are seven common **face shapes**. Being familiar with the different characteristics of each face shape will help you adapt hair designs to best suit your client. The majority of illustrations in this and upcoming portions of this lesson show women's faces because, in general, women's hair presents many more design options than men's hair. The same principles apply to men and women.

Oval

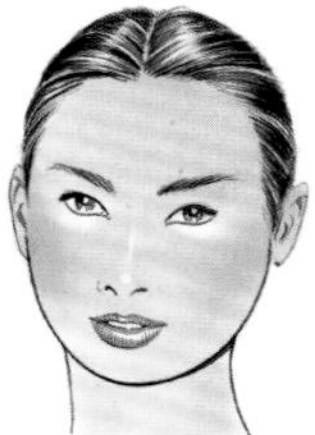

Round

Square

Oblong (Rectangle)

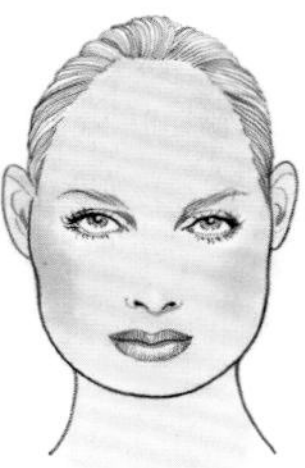

Pear (Trapezoid)

Diamond

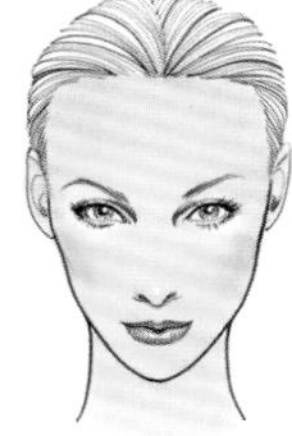

Heart (Triangle)

		DO	DON'T
OVAL 	The **oval face shape** is rounded, long and narrow rather than wide and short. » Standards of beauty change, but the oval facial shape is generally considered the ideal facial shape » Three sections of the face are in approximately equal proportions to one another » No dominant areas » Looks good with almost any hair design, length or texture » Sometimes lacks a particular point of interest; a stronger statement within the hair design may be used for interest	 Enhance features Balance body proportions	 Add too much height
The other face shapes can be balanced to create the illusion of a more harmonious oval shape.			
ROUND 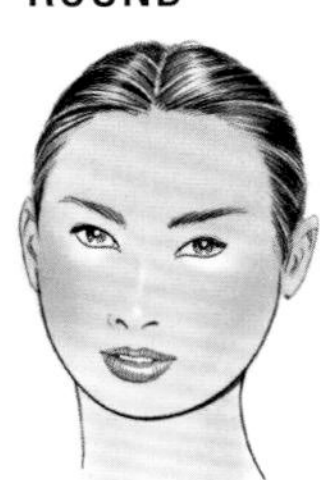	The **round face shape** looks circular and tends to look short and wide rather than long and narrow. This face often has a low, round hairline and a short chin with a rounded jawline. » Long, wispy side areas can help make cheeks look narrow » Looks good with a geometric, asymmetrical or linear hair design » Curls can emphasize roundness of face; if client has naturally curly hair, create an angular shape	 Add height to crown Add width below jawline or above temple Create angular shapes	 Add a full fringe Add width on sides Add equal fullness around entire face

SQUARE 	The **square face shape** is short, wide and angular with straight lines. The front hairline and jawline are almost horizontal with cheekbones that protrude very little on sides. » Looks good with hair designs that elongate face with height on top and narrowness at sides » Curly texture and wisps of hair around face can add softness to angular lines	**DO**  Sweep short hair up over ears Add soft movement to conceal square corners Begin side fullness at temples	**DON'T**  Add horizontal fringes or straight lines Add solid lines at jawline Add height without width Style hair straight/flat
OBLONG 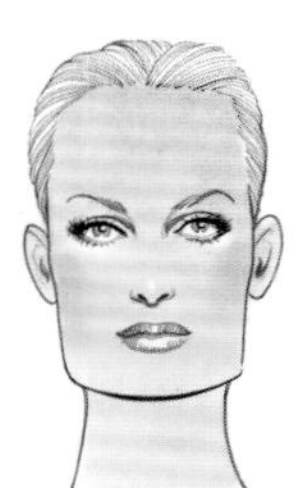	The **oblong (rectangle) face shape** is long, narrow and angular. The jawline is wide and almost horizontal. The hairline is only slightly curved. » One area of face may be longer (forehead, chin or middle section) » Cheekbones barely protrude, sometimes resulting in vertical-looking sides » Looks good with softness and width and longer, layered hair » Chin-length hair with volume on sides can be flattering » A fringe can shorten the look of the oblong face	**DO**  Add softness Keep short hair equally full on top and above ears Add width at sides Use a side parting and diagonal fringe	**DON'T** 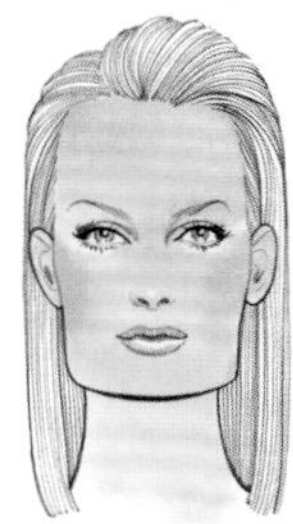 Style hair completely back away from the face Add height without width Keep hair long, flat and straight
PEAR 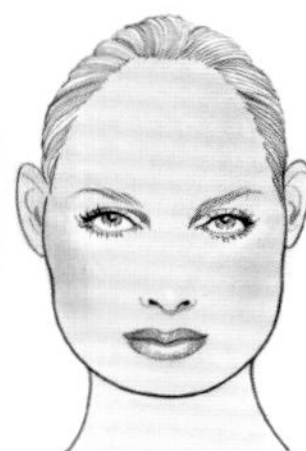	The **pear (trapezoid) face shape** is most often elongated, with a narrower forehead and a wide jaw. » Long, wispy side areas can slenderize cheeks and jaw » Look good with graduated forms; push volume up and above jawline into narrower areas » Avoid extremely short hair and designs with a solid form (bob) that ends at jawline	**DO**  Add volume above jawline Add height to crown; add width at forehead in short or medium styles Let long hair cover jawline to conceal its width	**DON'T**  Accentuate pear shape with narrowness at temples Accentuate pear shape with width at jawline

DIAMOND 	The **diamond face shape** appears elongated and angular. The widest area is at the cheekbones, while the forehead and chin are narrower. » Looks softer with narrow sides and fullness at chin » Looks good with short hair and longer, wispier nape lengths » Solid form (bob) hair sculptures work well	**DO**  Reduce width at sides Add width at forehead and jawline Use a side part and diagonal fringe	**DON'T**  Add width at cheekbones Add height on top Add short, cropped nape
HEART 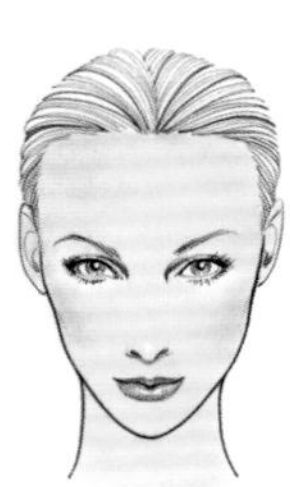	The **heart (triangle) face shape** is long and angular. The forehead is wider, while chin area is elongated and pointed. » Looks good with volume at jawline and little or no volume on top » Curls can help soften features » With shorter lengths, keep nape full	**DO**  Add width at jawline Leave fullness at nape that can be seen from front	**DON'T**  Add width at forehead or cheekbones Add diagonal-forward lines, long pointed side areas or cropped nape (too harsh)

SALON**CONNECTION**

Communicating Your Recommendations With Care!

The art of client communication includes finding the right words to encourage and support the client while making professional recommendations. The shape descriptions are intended to be a reference tool to facilitate learning and understanding, not as a way to label clients as you consult with them. For instance, instead of telling a client that they have a pear-shaped face, refer to fullness at the jaw and narrow forehead area. Remember, as people embrace their individuality, your efforts need to be focused on celebrating your clients' individual beauty, thus emphasizing their most attractive features. For more on speaking with clients, refer to the *Communicate With Confidence* and *Consult Service Essential* lessons.

PROFILE

A **profile** is an outline of an object from the side, especially the side view of the face and head. Hair designs should complement your client's profile as well as the front view. The most notable features of the profile are the:

- Forehead
- Nose
- Chin

Give your clients a hand-held mirror to help them view their profile as you make style recommendations. There are three different types of profiles:

1. **Straight**
2. **Convex**
3. **Concave**

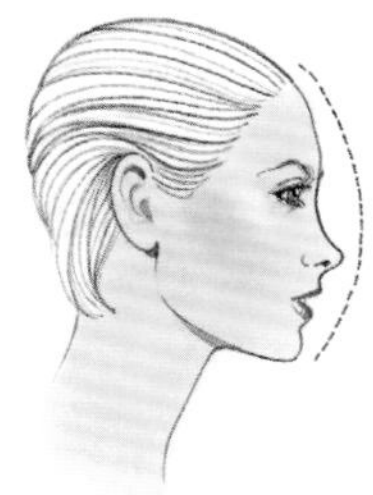

Straight Profile

A **straight profile** has a very slight outward curvature from the front hairline to the tip of the nose and from the tip of the nose to the chin.

- Considered ideal
- Can be left totally exposed by a hair design

Convex Profile

A **convex profile** has a strong or exaggerated outward curvature resulting from either a protruding nose or a sloping forehead or chin.

To create the illusion of a straight profile:

- Visually shorten length of nose
  - Add volume to fringe
  - Add volume to forehead
- Balance sloping chin
  - Keep shape of hair tighter in nape
  - Create a diagonal-forward perimeter line that points directly to chin
  - Camouflage receding chin on a male client with a full beard and mustache

Concave Profile

A **concave profile** has an inward curve, which is most often the result of a dominant, protruding forehead and chin, or a small nose.

To create the illusion of a straight profile:

- Compensate for dominant chin
  - Build fullness in nape
  - Avoid short nape lengths
  - Avoid diagonal-forward lines
- Cover large forehead
  - Sculpt a fringe and design it with minimal volume
- Compensate for smaller nose if forehead and/or chin are not also protruding
  - Move hair off and away from face

FACIAL FEATURES

Other features that may need special consideration when determining proper proportions include:

- Receding hairline
- Protruding ears
- Eyeglasses

Receding Hairline

- Avoid side part directly in center of recession area
- Design hair without any direct part
- Design hair so it falls slightly forward to cover receding area

Protruding Ears

- Cover with longer hair
- Add more volume and fullness at sides if hair is short

Eyeglasses

A client who wears eyeglasses may pose two different types of challenges:

- Giving advice on the type of frame shape to select
- Adapting the client's hair design to the glasses already being worn

In general, the client's face shape is the main factor that should guide the type of eyeglass frames that would best flatter the client and the same principles of proportion apply as in hair design. Selection of the eyeglass frames should also take into account:

- Client's overall body shape
- Personality
- Lifestyle
- Clothing preferences

When you keep the shape, size and color of the glasses in mind, you'll be better able to recommend an eyeglass design that works with your client's total image.

GUIDELINES FOR SELECTING EYEGLASSES

- Select large glasses for a larger face, small glasses for a smaller face.
- If client views glasses as a fashion accessory, suggest a pair that draws attention through shape or color.
- If client sees glasses as a necessity, suggest a delicate frame in gold or silver or possibly unframed lenses.
- The shape of the frame can enhance or compensate for the shape of the face.
- Square-shaped glasses can give a round face more interest; round pair of glasses can soften a square face; a wide frame can add width to a narrow face.
- Select an eyeglass frame color that corresponds to the tone of the client's coloring
- Cool-toned frames, such as silver, blue or teal, better suit clients with cool coloring; frames with warm colors, such as gold or crimson, flatter clients with warm coloring.

HAIR COLOR AND NATURAL COLORING

When consulting with clients who want to change their hair color and/or makeup, analyzing their natural coloring is an important first step.

The right hair color can:

- Emphasize natural skin tone
- Emphasize eye color
- Make client look fresher and more radiant

To determine which fashion colors are most flattering for your clients, analyze the pigmentation of their hair, skin, eyes and lips.

1. Determine whether the client's color scheme tends to be warm, cool or neutral

- Warm colors contain yellow, orange and/or red
- Cool colors contain blue, green and/or violet
- Neutral colors, such as browns, contain all three primary colors: yellow, red and blue

2. Determine intensity of those colors (mild or strong)

PIGMENTATION FACTORS

	WARM			COOL	
	MILD	STRONG	NEUTRAL	MILD	STRONG
HAIR					
Natural Hair Color					
Childhood Hair Color					
SKIN					
Scalp					
Skin Behind Ear					
Skin on Face					
Cheek Color					
Freckles on Arms and Shoulders					
Shadows Around Eyes					
EYES					
Eye Color					
Circle Around Eyes					
Whites of Eyes					
LIPS					
Natural Lip Color					
TOTAL:					

The following images show the influence that colors have on the client's overall look and whether they are chosen correctly or incorrectly. The first image shows the client without any makeup.

1. Analyze the skin color, eye color and lips.

2. Look at the other two images and note the positive and negative effects that colors have on the total image.

The hair color, as well as the makeup color, should parallel the client's natural coloring and intensity in order to emphasize the natural beauty.

Once you understand the relationship between hair designs and body/ facial shape, you can combine that knowledge with your clients' clothing and lifestyle choices to develop a complete look they will love.

Keep in mind that hair texture, density, condition and growth patterns all play a role in the design decision process. Refer to the lessons on *Hair Care* and *Design Connection* for more information.

CLOTHING AND LIFESTYLES

Clothing and lifestyle complement each other and need to be considered when designing the hair. Ask clients questions about their clothing style to get a full picture. Internationally, designers and the fashion industry identify six general clothing styles: casual, natural, classic, romantic, gamine and dramatic.

CLOTHING STYLES

CASUAL

- Like clothing and environment to be comfortable and low-maintenance
- Wardrobe includes flat, comfortable shoes, sneakers, blue jeans, T-shirts and sweatshirts
- Are practical and comfortable for elegant events
- Hair designs are easy to style and maintain
- Hair is often longer and worn in a loose ponytail
- Male clients prefer a low-maintenance haircut

NATURAL

- Wear colors and materials found in nature.
- Clothes often made from fabrics like cotton and wool
- Jewelry often made from stone and wood
- Low-maintenance hair designs that don't require many styling products
- Like hair to look and feel healthy
- Concerned about personal health, environment and animal testing when selecting salon products

CLASSIC

- Wardrobe is coordinated
- Every piece of clothing is well-chosen and exemplifies a traditional design look
- Clothing color selections often include navy, black, white, cream, beige, brown and gray
- Like hair well-designed and in good condition
- Natural hair color shades preferred, sometimes with thin highlights
- Like sophisticated short hair, classic solid form bobs
- Long hair often worn in a ponytail or bun
- Male clients keep hair short well-groomed

ROMANTIC

- Love silk, flower prints, lace, beads and pastel shades of color
- Clothing is often tone-on-tone
- Often wear vintage accessories, such as shawls and small, detailed jewelry
- Prefer hair designs that are soft
- Like curls and soft hair colors that may include golden blond, light brown and strawberry blond highlights

GAMINE

- Fashion-oriented and enjoy wearing latest looks
- Jewelry is small and often geometric in shape
- Prefer short hair
- Have an eye for interesting detail

DRAMATIC

- Gravitate to things that are out of the ordinary, draw attention and turn heads
- Like loud and colorful clothing and accessories
- Seek out change and embrace new and exciting ideas
- Not afraid to experiment with hair designs and colors that reflect their bold style
- Gives designer the opportunity to stretch their creativity

LIFESTYLE FACTORS

When making a design decision, it's important to take your client's lifestyle into account in order to determine a hair design's practicality. Some **lifestyle factors** to consider:

- Job/career
- Hobbies
- Family
- Time available
- Finances
- Hair care skills

Job/Career

Many clients spend most of their time at work; consider the following when making design decisions:

- Functional demands of their job
- Type of image job requires

Hobbies

Things clients do for fun, fitness or relaxation can affect their hair in different ways; ask clients whether their spare time activities will:

- Pose any restrictions
- Create needs for their hair that should be considered

Family

Ask clients direct questions about the following factors in order to clear up doubts and avoid later disappointment:

- Are their partner's and family's preferences important to them?
- Do they have small children, and if so, do they prefer a low-maintenence design?

Time

The amount of time a client is willing and able to spend on hair care can give you an immediate indication of how elaborate the hair design can be. Time will determine how much of the following is desired:

- Maintenance
- Products
- Tools

Finances

The costs involved with the client's selected design need to be made clear. Make sure the client has a full picture of what's to come ahead of time:

- Cost of initial design change
- Cost associated with ongoing maintenance
  - Recurring salon costs
  - At-home care

Skills

Even though clients may be willing to invest all the time and money necessary for a certain look, some clients may not have the skills to maintain it:

- Provide a through explanation of the proper tools or products for the client to use for home maintenance
- Demonstrate correct methods and techniques they can use to achieve the best results

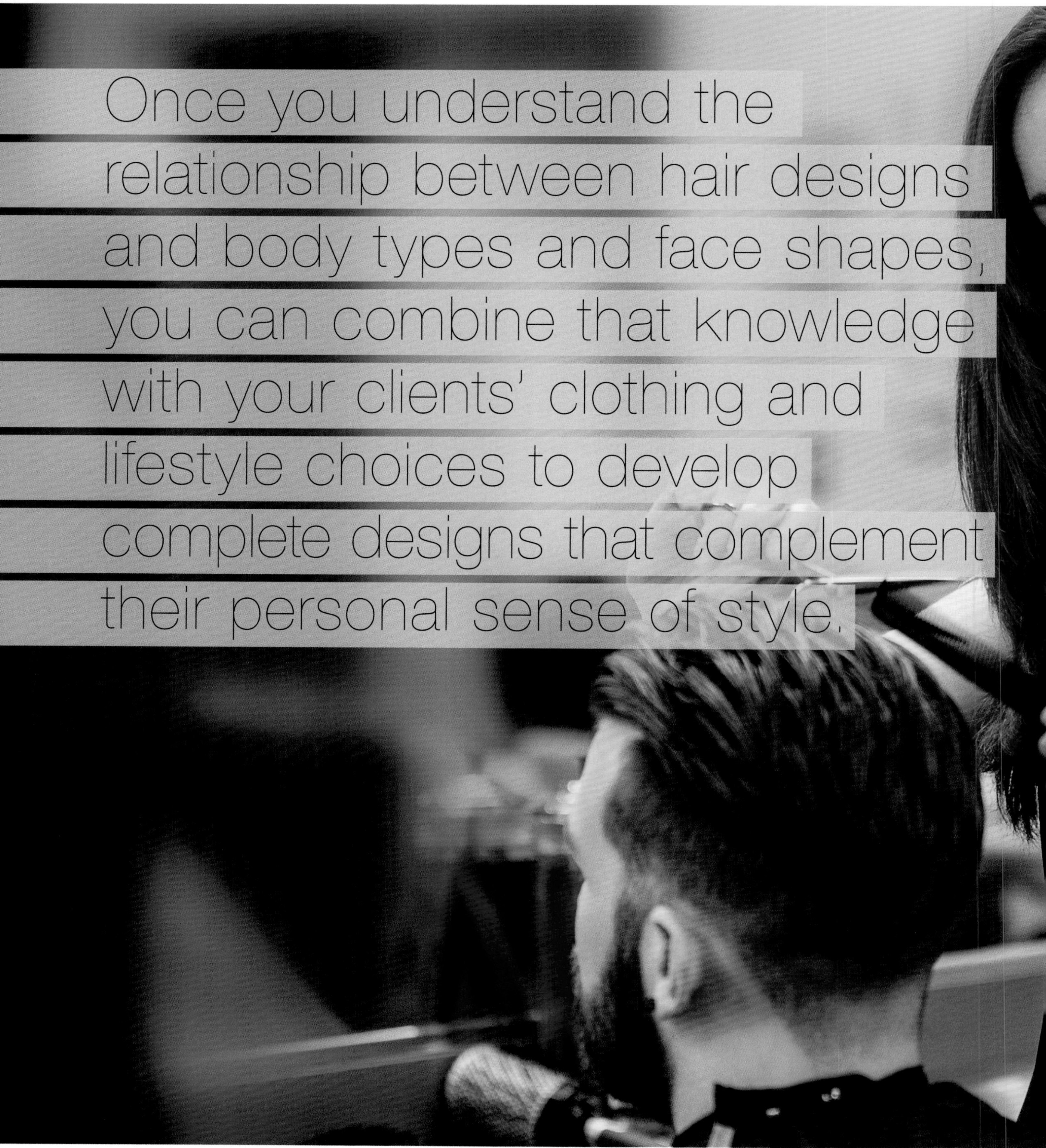
Once you understand the relationship between hair designs and body types and face shapes, you can combine that knowledge with your clients' clothing and lifestyle choices to develop complete designs that complement their personal sense of style.

LESSONS LEARNED

Hair designs can be adapted to complement different body types.

- Tall and lanky – Benefit from hair designs with added volume/and or length
- Rectangle-shaped – Can wear almost any hair length or type of design
- Short and sturdy – Benefit from hair designs with height and volume at the top

Body shapes include: hourglass, apple, triangle (pear), inverted triangle, rectangle

Hair design options that complement various face shapes include:

- Oval-shaped faces look good with almost any hair design, length or texture
- Round-shaped faces benefit from added height
- Square-shaped faces benefit from added height on top and narrowness at the sides
- Oblong-shaped faces benefit from width at the sides
- Pear-shaped faces benefit from added volume above the jawline into the narrow areas or upper crest area
- Diamond-shaped faces benefit from narrow sides and fullness at the chin
- Heart-shaped faces benefit from added volume at the chin and little or no volume on top

The six clothing styles to consider when making design decisions for your clients are:

- Casual
- Natural
- Classic
- Romantic
- Gamine
- Dramatic

Six lifestyle factors to consider when making design decisions for your clients include:

- Job/career
- Hobbies
- Family
- Time availability
- Finances
- Hair care skills

CONNECT SERVICE ESSENTIAL 104^{C}.3

EXPLORE //

Do you feel you have a genuine connection with people at businesses that you visit frequently?

INSPIRE //

Connecting with your client is the first step in delivering an exceptional service experience.

ACHIEVE //

Following this lesson on the *Connect Service Essential*, you'll be able to:

- List the four Service Essentials
- Demonstrate specific strategies for connecting with clients
- Discuss additional elements that affect how well you connect with clients
- Apply all five senses when using techniques to connect with clients

FOCUS //

CONNECT SERVICE ESSENTIAL

Connect Strategies

Connecting With the Five Senses

104°.3 | CONNECT SERVICE ESSENTIAL

Every contact you have with a client is an opportunity to distinguish yourself as a premier salon professional. There are four Service Essentials—4 Cs—that make up the service experience: Connect, Consult, Create and Complete. These are interactions between salon professionals and their clients that can create exceptional service experiences. This lesson explores the Connect service essential, the first of the 4 Cs.

SERVICE ESSENTIALS: THE 4 Cs
1. **Connect** Establishes rapport and builds credibility with each client
2. **Consult** Analyzes client wants and needs, visualizes the end result, organizes the plan for follow-through and obtains client consent
3. **Create** Produces functional, predictable and pleasing results
4. **Complete** Reviews the service experience and client satisfaction, offers product recommendations, expresses appreciation and provides follow-up

CONNECT STRATEGIES

Connect is the first Service Essential. When connecting with a client, the goal is to help them feel comfortable and confident with you and the salon service you are about to perform. Showing authentic interest, empathy and warmth toward the client is a good place to start.

The salon industry is built on positive connections between the professional and the client. These connections begin with a friendly greeting and continue throughout the service experience; it's the little things professionals do to make their clients feel comfortable.

Connect strategies help establish rapport and build credibility with each client. Here are some specific guidelines to help you connect with your clients and gain credibility:

1. Make Eye Contact, Smile and Say "Hello"

This is a simple way to ease your clients' tension.

- Try to greet your clients as soon as they arrive–within the first 10 seconds.
- If you are not able to begin service immediately, tell the client how long you will be. Offer magazines, food or beverages to make their wait more comfortable.

2. Use Your Client's Name

This will make every client feel like they're important to you.

- Start questions and statements using the client's name.
- When in doubt, ask the client how to pronounce their name so you'll be sure to say it correctly.

3. Introduce Yourself to Your Client

This is extremely important for first-time clients to gain their confidence.

- Find a greeting that works for you and customize it.
- If appropriate, shake hands.
- Be friendly, warm and inviting in your words and tone.
- Use poised, calm movements to project confidence and competence.
- Keep your attention focused completely on the client.

4. Give the Client Helpful Direction

The more informed they are, the more comfortable your client will feel.

- Don't assume they know what to do or where to go.
- Explain where you are going, what to expect and what you are going to do. For example:
  - Invite clients back to the design area or treatment room.
  - Help them take their coat off and offer to put it away until the service is done.
  - Walk next to them and make polite conversation.
  - Actively maintain clients' safety and comfort. For instance, at your workstation, turn the chair toward the aisle and hold it until the client is seated; then turn the chair back to the mirror, elevate and secure it.

> "To keep a customer demands as much skill as to win one."
> —American proverb

Left Hanging

Have you ever entered a restaurant and after you told the host or hostess the number in your party, they walked away without saying anything? Did you follow them, or wait for them to come back? Ever followed them and had them turn around, only to bump into you? This situation can be awkward and uncomfortable for the customer.

In the salon, be sure to let your clients know what to do and where to go immediately after you greet them.

- If there is a designated place for coats and/or personal items, direct them to that area or take the items for them.
- Let them know immediately if they should follow you back to your workstation or if they should remain up front until you return for them.
- In addition to offering food or drinks when available, let clients know where the bathroom is located.

Small things like this ensure your clients feel comfortable and at ease right away and help the connecting process move along smoothly.

Your communication skills will play a big role in how well you connect with clients. Review the *Basic Communication* and *Communicate With Confidence* lessons for some useful tips and techniques. In addition to communication skills, some other factors that affect your ability to connect with clients include:

Personality – Your own personality tendencies, the personality tendencies of your clients and how they interrelate	» The more you observe your clients' actions and language, the more you'll understand their personality tendencies. » Adapting the way you communicate based on your client's personality tendencies will help you establish rapport and maintain good client relationships.
Schedule/Time – The impact that time pressures and scheduling constraints can have on communication	» Variables that affect your time include whether the client is new or repeat, the type of service being performed and the number of services scheduled for the day. » For first-time clients, allow ample time to connect, as this will set the tone for your ongoing relationship. » Even when a previous appointment runs late, don't shorten or omit your connecting time with the next client.
Environment – How elements within the immediate environment can help or hinder effective communication	» Minimize distraction and make sure you always have your client's full attention. » Keep interpersonal conflicts off the salon floor. » Make sure music and reading material in waiting area are appropriate so that clients are relaxed and comfortable.
Professional Appearance – The effect that your appearance and hygiene can have on client perceptions	» Your appearance is often immediately connected to the client's expectations of your job performance; a professional look will inspire trust and confidence from clients. » Monitor your personal hygiene–bad breath, unkempt clothing, hair and nail grooming and body odors–as others may be reluctant to point out these things that clients might find off-putting.

Build a YES Momentum

Getting your client to say "yes" often in the beginning of the appointment helps build a "YES momentum." Gaining your client's permission to do little things, like following you to the design area or accepting a beverage, sets the tone for gaining their agreement to bigger things. Establish a "yes" habit early on in the appointment.

SALON**CONNECTION**

Front Desk Etiquette

Whether it's a new client or a repeat client, the way that person feels while they're in your salon determines whether they will choose to buy your products and services again next week, next month or next year. The client's experience starts as soon as they enter the salon. The following are additional guidelines for salon professionals at the front desk.

- Acknowledge all clients when they arrive—even just to let them know you'll be with them shortly.
- Don't allow bad moods to carry over into conversations with clients.
- Don't share personal opinions that are not positive.
- Don't eat, drink or chew gum on the phone or at the desk.
- Don't talk about one client in front of another client; avoid holding side conversations.
- Don't ignore requests, even if you are busy.
- Offer more than one-word answers.
- Avoid saying "No problem." Some feel this is a negative phrase that transforms their gratitude into debt and apology; it suggests that they may have inconvenienced you in some way.
- Always say "Please," "Thank you," "You're welcome," "My pleasure" and "I'm happy to help."

CONNECTING WITH THE FIVE SENSES

There are several techniques that can help you connect with your clients. Using all five senses will ensure that their salon visit is exceptionally memorable.

Sight: In addition to your personal appearance, keep your workstation clean. Consider gender-neutral colors for capes and other personal décor so that male clients feel just as comfortable as female clients.

Sound: Background music is a big part of the salon's ambiance. Be conscious of the sound level and the varied tastes of your clientele. Make sure you speak with a friendly tone and make an effort to be warm and sincere in your communication.

Touch: In a survey of 2,000 salon clients, the majority said their favorite thing about their service experience was getting a shampoo. Clients like to feel pampered. A nice shampoo or scalp massage can go a long way to helping a client feel relaxed and comfortable in your capable hands.

Smell: The products you use on your clients, hopefully, will have a pleasant smell. The lingering scents work to your advantage when suggesting purchases. Also, a soft fragrance on your wrists can be pleasing to the client in your chair, as your hands and arms are constantly in motion around their face as you perform services.

Taste: Offer your client something to drink upon arrival and at some point during the service if appropriate. Refreshments are a small way to show your clients how much you appreciate their business and to entice them to come back.

DISCOVER**MORE**

Consistency Helps You Connect

One of the most important things you can do to connect with existing clients is to be consistent in your routine each time they visit.

- If you offered them coffee or tea the last time they visited, be sure to offer them coffee or tea the next time you see them.
- Make sure the same type of reading material is always available for clients waiting for services.
- Always greet clients with a smile and show the same level of enthusiasm each time.

Consistency in these areas helps relax the client because they know exactly what to expect each time they visit your salon.

You can also keep a client record—print or digital—to get to know your clients. Write down facts about your clients like birthdays and what services they like best. Listen to what they have to say and write a few notes on ways you can improve your client's service experience. Review this shortly before they come in to see you each time.

LESSONS LEARNED

- The four Service Essentials are Connect, Consult, Create and Complete.
- To connect with clients, some good strategies are to make eye contact, use the client's name, introduce yourself and give helpful direction throughout the service.
- Personality differences between you and the client, your schedule/available time, your environment and your professional appearance all have an effect on how well you connect with your clients.
- Clean workstations and professional appearance, background music, pampering with shampoo and massages, pleasant aromas and refreshments are a few ways you can connect with your clients and enhance their experience through all five senses.

104^{C}.4 CONSULT

SERVICE ESSENTIAL

INSPIRE //

A client consult helps you understand exactly what the client wants and ensures your service meets those expectations.

EXPLORE //

Have you ever given someone instructions for a task, but it didn't turn out like you wanted?

ACHIEVE //

Following this lesson on the *Consult Service Essential*, you'll be able to:

- Discuss the four strategies that make up the Consult Service Essential
- Give examples of how you can connect with clients during the consultation
- Summarize the importance of keeping updated client records

FOCUS //

CONSULT SERVICE ESSENTIAL

Consult Strategies

Consultations Help You Connect

Consultation Records

104ᶜ.4 | CONSULT SERVICE ESSENTIAL

You've greeted your client and made a connection; it's time to move on to the second Service Essential: Consult. During this step, you will discuss the specifics of your client's service and explain how you plan to achieve their desired result. You'll listen as your client communicates what they want; then work with them to develop a plan of action to ensure you both understand what the final result will be and feel good about it.

SERVICE ESSENTIALS: THE 4 Cs
1. **Connect** Establishes rapport and builds credibility with each client
2. **Consult** Analyzes client wants and needs, visualizes the end result, organizes the plan for follow-through and obtains client consent
3. **Create** Produces functional, predictable and pleasing results
4. **Complete** Reviews the service experience and client satisfaction, offers product recommendations, expresses appreciation and provides follow-up

"Good service is good business."
—Siebel Ad

CONSULT STRATEGIES

Consulting with your client is a four-step process that includes:

1. Analyzing the client's wants and needs
2. Visualizing the end results
3. Organizing the plan for follow-through
4. Obtaining client consent

1. Analyze the Client's Wants and Needs

Depending on the service offered, salon professionals might analyze the shape of the head and face, the current condition and color of the skin, or the health and shape of the natural nails.

- Analyze client's hair and scalp and check for any contraindications.
- Gather facts about your client's lifestyle, maintenance preferences and budget considerations.
- Analyze the client's physical attributes, such as body type, facial shape and natural hair scheme.
- Look and listen for cues and clues the client sends throughout the consultation:
  - Touching their hair, skin or nails in the areas that cause frustration
  - Saying things like "I hate this," or "When I have a bad hair day, it does this," or "I wish my hair [skin or nails] would do/look like this."
- Ask open-ended questions that can't be answered with just a "yes" or "no," to determine what the client wants to achieve.
  - Open-ended questions usually begin with who, what, where, why, when or how.
  - It's helpful to use two categories: "Want" questions help uncover what clients want that they currently don't have. "Have" questions help uncover problems or challenges clients currently have.

"WANT" QUESTIONS

"Want" questions help uncover what clients want that they currently don't have.

What final results do you want to see in your hair [skin or nails]?

Listen to hear the client use "want" words, such as:

HAIR	SKIN	NAILS
Shine	Smooth	Smooth
Warmth	Clear	Shaped
Fullness	Soft	Shine
Body	Healthy	Strong
Healthy		
Movement		

"HAVE" QUESTIONS

"Have" questions help uncover problems or challenges guests currently have.

What types of problems or challenges do you have with your hair [skin or nails]?

Listen to hear the client use "have" words, such as:

HAIR	SKIN	NAILS
Dull	Dry	Drab
Lifeless	Shiny	Chipped
Limp	Discolored	Brittle
Flat	Breaking out	Split
Flyaway	Oily	Thin
Won't stay		Thick

> "Your customer doesn't care how much you know until they know how much you care."
> —Damon Richards

A great question to ask new clients during a consultation is how they found your salon. This provides an opening for the client to provide some background on their previous experience with other salon professionals. It's obvious that they are looking for a change; understanding why will help you give them the outstanding service they are looking for and hopefully make them a return client.

2. Visualize the End Results

Salon professionals need to visualize the possibilities that will enhance the client's appearance or well-being.

- Hairstylists analyze the elements of form, texture and color and the interplay of design principles like repetition, alternation, progression and contrast.
- Estheticians analyze the color and/or contour patterns for a makeup application.
- Nail technicians analyze the shape and color of the finished nail design.

In many instances, clients bring a photo to show the look they want. Study it and ask yourself:

- What type of haircut [skin or nail care] is needed to achieve this look?
- What type of chemical service or treatment was used to achieve this look?
- What products were used to achieve this look?
- What additional services were used to achieve this overall look–highlights? Eyebrows? Makeup? Nail art?

You may want to use a style selector that shows examples of the diverse services offered within the salon.

3. Organize the Plan for Follow-Through

- Organize the information you've gathered from speaking with your client and the analysis you made using your own observations.
- Once you see the final result in your mind, consider the procedures, techniques, products and tools you will use.
- Share a brief summary with the client and explain the need for any additional services if required to create the desired results; upselling becomes a natural process when your clients desire a particular look.

4. Obtain Client Consent

Gaining consent, or agreement, helps the client feel in control.

- After you've discussed the client's wants, continue the consultation with questions like "May I make some suggestions?" or "May I share some ideas?"
- Help them see the link between the results they want and the services you'll need to perform.
- Explain everything in detail; ask your client if they have any questions about any part of the service, and clarify it for them if necessary.
- Gain feedback from the client and explain the cost of upkeep and home care for the style.
- If you sense hesitation, ask additional questions to clarify what the client really wants.
- As you gain consent to move forward, ensure that costs for the service have been explained and timeframes are clear.

Paraphrase to close the gap between what your clients are saying and your understanding of what they really mean. The best way to confirm that you truly understand what your client is trying to communicate is by repeating what they said back to them using your own words.

"Kind words can be short and easy to speak, but their echoes are truly endless."
—Mother Teresa

CONSULTATIONS HELP YOU CONNECT

During the Consult Service Essential, personality, time and environment also play a part in how well you communicate with the client. Just like the Connect essential, the Consult essential is extremely important for new clients. If your clients feel that you are really listening to them, they are more likely to return and recommend you to friends and family.

- Be honest with the client; maintain a kind smile and a reassuring tone. If you can't give the client what they want, be sure to say so and explain why; offer a positive alternative rather than a flat-out "no."
- Be sure to schedule enough time to consult before the service; schedule extra time for new clients.
- Make sure your consultation area offers enough privacy that the client feels comfortable sharing any confidential information.
- Make sure the noise level is minimal and the lighting is good in the area where you have chosen to consult with your client.
- When consulting, use visual aids to help the client communicate and explain what they want; these could include a color chart or color swatches, photos, design books/selectors, a full-body mirror, etc.

SALON**CONNECTION**

Gaining the Client's Trust

Many clients don't understand their hair's texture, growth patterns, or how facial shape relates to and influences a hair design. Explaining some of these during the consultation can help you gain agreement faster about how the final results of the service should look. Sharing your knowledge will let the client know they are in good hands.

As a salon professional, you will learn a lot of personal information about your clients. They need to be able to trust you and count on your discretion. If that trust is broken, it can damage your reputation as well as the salon's. Client records/info and personal information they share with you should be confidential. These records belong to the salon, and you should not look at or alter records without appropriate permission.

CONSULTATION RECORDS

Most salons will keep some form of client records–either printed or digital. In addition to basic contact information for the client, these documents should contain relevant information in regard to the client's health and details of the agreed-upon services/treatment plans.

Keeping these records updated is important because hair, skin and nails change over time. Recording these details ensures that any staff member in the salon will be able to meet this client's service needs safely and effectively. It also serves as a record of how any long-term treatments or services are progressing.

A few things to keep in mind:

- Do not leave records in view where anybody can read them.
- Keep all records safely secured and/or put away.
- Refer to client records before each consultation/visit with the client.
- Update the client records at the end of the consultation and/or service.

Tips for a Successful Consultation

1. Listen to your client attentively and maintain eye contact throughout the consultation.
2. Sit next to your client during the consultation so they don't have to look up at you.
3. Ask the client what they like about their hair/skin/nails and find out how they care for it.
4. Establish what your client's hair concerns are, then tailor the conversation throughout the service around how/what products will resolve problems.
5. Add any relevant notes to the client consultation card or records, and update your client records regularly.

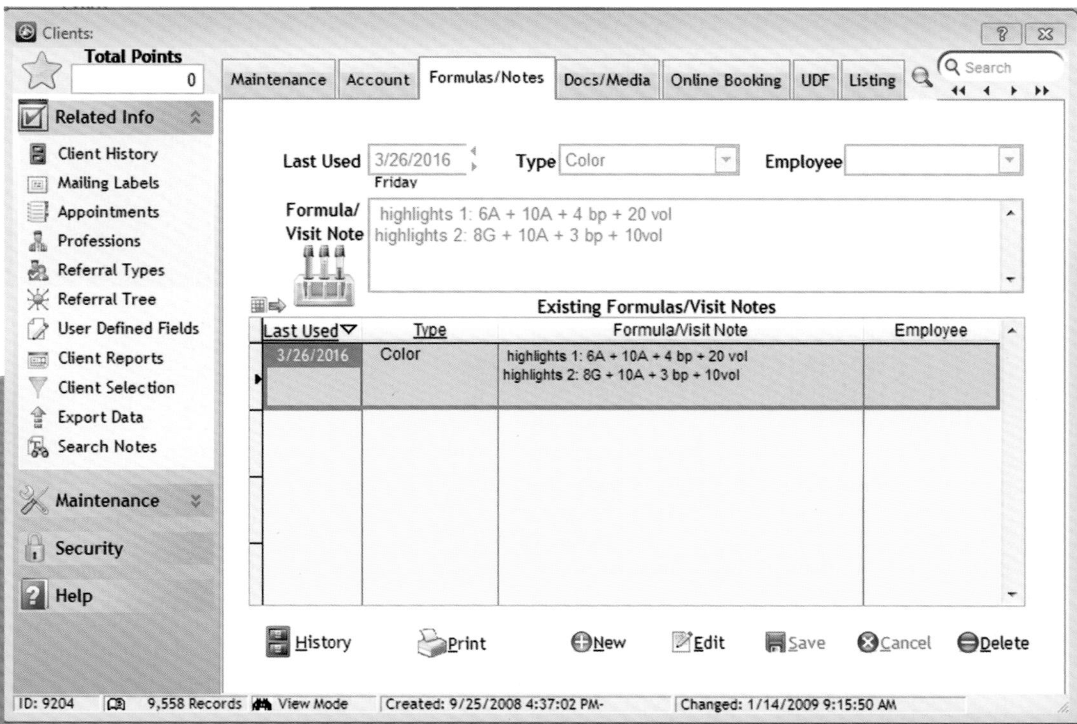

LESSONS LEARNED

- The four strategies that make up the Consult Service Essential are:
  - Analyzing the client's wants and needs
  - Visualizing the end results
  - Organizing the plan for follow-through
  - Obtaining client consent
- Connect with your clients during the consultation by being honest; allowing ample time for the consultation; making sure the consultation area is private, quiet and well-lit; and using visual aids to help you better understand what the client wants.
- Client records are important because they allow salon professionals to monitor the changes to a client's hair/skin/nails over time and ensure that any staff member will be able to provide safe and efficient services when needed.

104°.5 // CREATE

SERVICE ESSENTIAL

EXPLORE //

When artists are creating, do they start with the end result in mind? Do they adapt and improvise along the way?

INSPIRE //

Providing your clients with a memorable service experience leads to return clients and referrals.

ACHIEVE //

Following this lesson on the *Create Service Essential*, you'll be able to:

- List the three most important steps in the Create essential
- Explain the difference between features and benefits of products
- Give examples of how to make each client's service exceptional
- Identify ways you can help customize a service for every client

FOCUS //

CREATE SERVICE ESSENTIAL

Create Strategies

Make the Client Experience Count

104^{c}.5 | CREATE SERVICE ESSENTIAL

The third Service Essential—Create—involves performing the service on your client and explaining what you are doing along the way. Use your technical skills and strategies learned from the previous Service Essentials to meet or exceed your client's expectations.

SERVICE ESSENTIALS: THE 4 Cs
1. **Connect** Establishes rapport and builds credibility with each client
2. **Consult** Analyzes client wants and needs, visualizes the end result, organizes the plan for follow-through and obtains client consent
3. **Create** Produces functional, predictable and pleasing results
4. **Complete** Reviews the service experience and client satisfaction, offers product recommendations, expresses appreciation and provides follow-up

> “Your smile is your logo, your personality is your business card, how you leave others feeling after having an experience with you becomes your trademark.”
>
> —Jay Danzie

CREATE STRATEGIES

The Create Service Essential produces functional, predictable and pleasing results. The most important steps of the Create Service Essential are show, tell and teach. As you perform the service on your client, use products in an economical way, explain the steps and actions that are taking place, and recommend products, tools and techniques for follow-up care. Additionally, check your client's comfort and maintain a pleasant rapport while you work.

Pay close attention to your client's facial expressions and body language. A smile or a nod is a sign that the client likes what you are doing or have just completed. This is a good time to educate the client on how to achieve the same results at home. A few things to keep in mind:

- Make the education process fun; this portion of the service experience is about teaching, not selling.
- Introduce each technique as quick and easy.
- Don't criticize or lose your patience.
- Do not perform services the client cannot recreate or maintain at home unless it's a one-time service for a special event.
- Put the brush in the client's hand and show exactly where to position the blow dryer.
- For skin and nail care services, explain the correct sequence of steps and show how much of the product to use.
- Document products and services discussed with the client for future reference.

Show—Tell—Teach

Show the client what you're doing:

"See how using a medium-size round brush gives you lift at the scalp?"
"Let me show you in the mirror how the warm mist of the facial steamer opens the pores of your skin for cleansing."
"This is a liquid nail wrap I will use to protect and harden your nails."
"I'm using deeper pressure here to release the tense spot in your muscle."

Tell the client what product/tool you are using and why:

"I am applying a gel to create a wet-look finish."
"I am using a medium fan brush to apply and blend the blush."
"I am using a top coat to prevent the polish from chipping."
"I am applying a heated cream to ensure a smooth massage motion."

Teach the client how to maintain the look at home:

"Push your hair back from the front hairline as you apply the pomade."
"Apply a small amount of the toner to this area first, followed by your forehead and chin."
"Use one brushstroke down the center of your nail followed by a stroke on each side of the nail surface."
"Use the massage cream sparingly, starting at your shoulder and moving to the crook of your elbow."

> "Being on par in terms of price and quality only gets you into the game. Service wins the game."
> —Tony Alessandra

FEATURES AND BENEFITS

As you teach clients about the products they need, share some information about each product. Focus mainly on the benefits of the products and briefly explain their features.

- A **feature** of a product is its characteristics or what's in it: natural bristles, vitamin E and almond oil are product features.
- A **benefit** of a product is what it does: adds shine, reduces frizz, strengthens, protects and relaxes.

Clients are most concerned with product results; if they are going to invest in a product, they want to know that it's going to work. When discussing product benefits, include:

- What the product does, its quality and convenience
- How the client's hair, skin or nails will look and feel after using the product
- What clients will gain from using the product, and what they will lose if they do not use the product

MAKE THE CLIENT EXPERIENCE COUNT

In a market where competitors offer the same products and services, the customer experience is what makes a salon stand out and can lead to customer loyalty. Beyond just repeat business, a great experience will generate referrals, and clients often are willing to pay more for consistently superior services. Here are a few tips adapted from *Behind the Chair* on how to make your clients feel they've had an exceptional visit:

1. **Pay special attention to your best customers.**

» Write down the names of your five favorite clients on the schedule each week; list ways you can make their experience more pleasurable.

» Suggest add-on services that enhance an existing cut or color.

» Suggest/create ways clients can style their hair differently.

2. **Provide knowledge.**

» Teach clients how to do their hair at home; make sure they're comfortable using the tools and products you recommend.

» Show them new ways to style their hair using different styling products, which will increase your retail sales.

» Talk to clients about classes you've attended and share your enthusiasm for new techniques or ways to approach hair/nail/skin care challenges.

3. **Use various relaxation techniques to care for clients.**

» During shampooing, make scalp massage a ritual that clients enjoy and appreciate.

» For men, provide a hot-towel facial experience during the appointment.

» When estheticians or nail technicians aren't busy, they can visit the floor and provide hand massages.

4. **Make the extras special and extraordinary.**

» Gaining agreement helps the client feel in control.

» Offer free fringe trims and neck trims for clients any time.

» Offer additional food and drinks besides the expected coffee or tea. Some salons are BYOB.

» Play upbeat or relaxing music–depending on the culture and vibe of your salon–and develop ways to engage your clients' senses of smell, taste and touch.

SALON**CONNECTION**

New Client Cape

Treating first-time clients like VIPs is a great way to ensure they have a memorable experience. One way to be sure new clients get special attention is to have them wear a different color cape. When any staff member sees a person wearing a different color cape, they know to be extra generous with a warm welcome, smiles and friendly comments. Paying attention to small details like this will make a big difference for each new client.

CUSTOMIZING EACH SERVICE EXPERIENCE

As with the first two Service Essentials, personality, time, environment and professional appearance all play a part in how well you connect with your client during the Create essential. During this part of the service, it's important to focus on your client and look for opportunities to exceed their expectations.

- Put yourself in the client's shoes and be sensitive to their needs: How do you like to be treated? Would you want your hair or nails to look like this?
- If the client wants to change or add a service, check with the front desk to ensure you have the time available.
- Put your mobile phone and other personal technology devices away while working on the salon floor; checking calls and social media is distracting for both you and your client.
- Keep fresh towels available to wipe the client's skin and brush hair off the client's neck and clothing to keep them comfortable during the service.
- Keep your workstation and surrounding work area clean and organized. Make sure all items to be used during the service are available and ready *before* you begin working on your client.

DISCOVER**MORE**

Retaining Male Clients

Some experts believe that men are more likely than women to return to a salon because of the experience they had. This makes creating an exceptional experience for male clients even more important. Here are a few suggestions on how to make that happen with each visit:

- Always give men a shampoo after a haircut; rinsing away the loose hairs will leave them feeling clean and refreshed.
- When suggesting styling products, use terms that are easy to understand, like *matte, gloss, firm* and *loose.*
- Try to use language men are comfortable with when discussing services. If you want to give him a manicure, call it *hand detailing*; instead of wispy, say *deconstructed*.
- Salon owners should strive to keep their shop gender-neutral. Avoid pink and floral patterns; keep a few men's magazines in the waiting room; carry products specifically for men.

The type of service you are performing and the preferences/desires of each client will help identify additional ways to enhance the service experience. The following chart discusses a few good places to start when determining ways to make your client's visit more memorable.

MAKE MEMORABLE VISITS

Listen.

- For many clients, a salon visit can be a form of therapy. A good salon professional listens to everything the client has to say.
- Maintain a relaxed ambiance that de-stresses your client.
- Some clients like to talk, and some may just want to relax.
- Watch and listen for verbal and nonverbal cues to determine what type of client is in your chair.

Keep the conversation professional.

- Try to avoid topics like religion, money, sex, romance or politics, even if the client brings them up.
- Don't talk about yourself too much or gossip about the salon and its employees. Instead, ask the client a few questions to get them talking about themselves.

Work with intent and focus.

- Maintain focus as you're performing the service.
- Stand back and check the balance and weight distribution of the style.
- Put your hands into the hair and move it around to check balance, proportion, weight and response.
- Learn from your work by cutting a section and evaluating what it did when it fell back into place.
- These actions will improve your techniques and help familiarize yourself with your clients' different hair types and textures.

Keep your work simple and make it repeatable.

- A good haircut, makeup application or manicure should look just as good when the client isn't in the salon as it did while they sat in your chair.
- Clients will appreciate a quick "how-to" session on recreating and maintaining their look.

Know your products.

- Product knowledge will help you select the best tools and products to correct any problems your client might be having.
- Being able to enhance the client's look will depend on product knowledge.

Remember that you are limited by the client's desires.

- Salon professionals may enjoy a certain level of artistic integrity, but your goal is to make the client look and feel beautiful according to their wants and needs–not just yours.
- Help the client understand what is doable and realistic.

"Customers are no longer buying products and services—they are buying experiences delivered via the products and services."
—Gregory Yankelovich

When the service is exceptional, clients will remain loyal to the salon and often refer others to come in for the experience.

LESSONS LEARNED

- The most important steps to follow during the Create essential are:
  - Show the client what you're doing.
  - Tell the client what product/tool you're using and why.
  - Teach the client how to maintain the look at home.
- A feature of a product is its characteristics or what's in it; a benefit of a product is what it does.
- You can provide exceptional service to your clients by paying special attention to your best customers, providing knowledge about products and at-home care, using relaxation techniques to make clients more comfortable and making the extras extraordinary.
- To better customize services for each client, you should listen, keep the conversation professional, work with intent and focus, keep your work simple and repeatable, know your products and remember that you are limited by the client's desires.

COMPLETE

SERVICE ESSENTIAL 104ᶜ.6

EXPLORE //

Ever watch what you thought was a great movie, up until the end? Did the bad ending ruin the entire movie for you?

INSPIRE //

Completing each service with appropriate advice and recommendations can mean more money plus new and return clients.

ACHIEVE //

Following this lesson on the *Complete Service Essential*, you'll be able to:

- Discuss strategies for solidifying your client relationship during the Complete Service Essential
- Explain the best approach to recommending products and after-care advice
- Give examples of ways to get feedback about client satisfaction

FOCUS //

COMPLETE SERVICE ESSENTIAL

Complete Strategies

After-Care Advice

104c.6 | COMPLETE SERVICE ESSENTIAL

Complete is the fourth and final Service Essential. Think of completing a salon or spa experience as your opportunity to provide a "big finish" for your clients—a memorable ending to their visit. After you have put so much effort into creating an exceptional experience during the Connect, Consult and Create Service Essentials, you don't want to ruin it by having clients leave on a sour, impersonal note.

SERVICE ESSENTIALS: THE 4 Cs
1. **Connect** Establishes rapport and builds credibility with each client
2. **Consult** Analyzes client wants and needs, visualizes the end result, organizes the plan for follow-through and obtains client consent
3. **Create** Produces functional, predictable and pleasing results
4. **Complete** Reviews the service experience and client satisfaction, offers product recommendations, expresses appreciation and provides follow-up

At this stage of the service, you are reviewing the visit, making sure the client has everything they needs to maintain their look at home, and ending the visit in a way that ensures they will be back again.

Solidify your relationship with your client by:

- Reinforcing the client's satisfaction with their overall experience
- Making professional product recommendations
- Prebooking the client's next appointment(s)
- Ending with a warm goodbye
- Providing follow-up after the salon visit

Hopefully, by the time you get to this part of the visit, clients have had an exceptional experience and feel that their time with you has made a positive impact on their lives. Helping clients look and feel their best is key to creating an exceptional experience for them. It's at this time, when clients are expressing their gratitude and appreciation, you should ask for referrals.

COMPLETE STRATEGIES

1. **Reinforce Client Satisfaction**

After you have created the results you and your client agreed to, review the overall experience to be sure the client is satisfied.

- Don't assume your client sees the result the same way you do; if something small is bothering them, it might make a world of difference if you knew about it and corrected it.
- Briefly summarize the services you performed with emphasis on the positive changes and benefits.
- Prompt the client to tell you how they feel about what has been accomplished.
- Ask questions and look for verbal and nonverbal cues to determine your client's level of satisfaction; fix what can be fixed right away (if applicable).
- If there is a significant problem, make every effort to schedule another appointment quickly so it can be corrected.
- Remind clients how great their hair, skin or nails look, and especially how great their total appearance looks.

2. **Make Professional Product Recommendations**

During the entire service process, your clients have been paying attention as you give advice on what products and tools will help them achieve and maintain the look or feel they want for their hair, skin or nails.

- Summarize the products you have already discussed and recommended, and ask if they are interested in taking those products home.
- If the client says no, keep your composure and try not to say anything that would embarrass or offend the client. Try something like: "That's fine. I'll just make a note of what we talked about. That way, if you change your mind, we'll have a record of the products we used."
- Ask the client for retail and referrals at the end of the appointment prior to escorting them to the front desk; it's likely they may lose interest in what you are saying once at the front desk because their focus has shifted.
- Use retail strategies such as offering samples, providing alternative choices in type and size of product, and including a gift with purchase.

"It's easy to make a buck. It's a lot tougher to make a difference."
—Tom Brokaw

3. **Prebook Client's Next Appointment**

Prebooking is one of the best techniques for turning first-time clients into return clients. They may have enjoyed the experience and liked the results they got, but if you don't complete the visit by scheduling a new appointment, you can't be certain you'll see them again.

- Now is a good time to check the client record for profile accuracy, particularly if you send reminders for the next appointment.
- Open your calendar and direct your client's attention to five weeks from today's date—or whatever timeframe is appropriate; try to offer two different appointment times to help your client make a convenient choice.
- Confer with the front desk to reserve the time.

4. **End With a Warm Goodbye**

Many successful salon professionals view their clientele as an extension of their friendship network. They welcome the opportunity to give clients a warm goodbye and look forward to seeing them again.

- Complete the service in the scheduled time.
- If you have not already started your next appointment, end the visit while walking your client to the door.
- If you have already started with your next client, do your best to graciously thank your last client while maintaining contact with your current client.
- The end of the salon visit should be as personal and engaging as the beginning of the visit.

5. **Complete Client Record**

- Include any contraindications and recommended products.
- List any changes in procedure or formulas.

6. **Provide Follow-Up After the Salon Visit**

Follow-up calls after the salon visit, reminder cards to prompt the next salon visit, thank-you-for-the-recent-visit cards, newsletters, emails and birthday cards are all ways to show clients you care. These strategies are among the easiest ways to build the goodwill that makes clients return.

- Few salon professionals make follow-up calls, even in problem situations that may demand it; this will set you apart from the competition.
- A client with a first-ever perm, chemical peel or set of acrylic nails, for instance, would likely feel an extra degree of comfort after getting a call from a professional who wants to make sure everything is okay.
- By calling your clients to make sure they are happy, you get a second chance to address any problems they might not have mentioned during the salon visit.
- Your call will make them feel important; without follow-up, even the most satisfied and loyal clients may not return.

Thank-You Cards
Thank-you cards range from friendly, warm designs to more formal, businesslike formats. Even humorous thank-you cards are sometimes used to show appreciation. Generally, a hand-addressed envelope adds a personal touch to the card. Your clients will definitely notice—and appreciate—that you took the extra time to add that personal touch.

The Complete Service Essential need not take a lot of time, but don't neglect it since it can reinforce the positive relationship developed throughout the service. However, if rushed, it can cause more damage than good. Recommend products for the client to take home, but be careful not to push. If you are late for your next appointment, do only as much as you can do calmly and respectfully, but always let the client know that you appreciated his or her visit and continued patronage.

AFTER-CARE ADVICE

Giving after-care advice to clients and recommending products they can use to care for their hair, skin and nails between visits to the salon is becoming an increasingly important part of the salon professional's job. Be careful not to make negative comments about other products. Staying in the positive vibe will help keep the service exceptional and memorable.

When doing this, you should spell out the benefits of using the product at home. Explain to your client:

- Which product you have used on their hair/skin/nails
- Why you have used it
- When and how they should use it

The next time your client comes into the salon, be sure to ask if they were happy with the product and able to maintain their look.

SALON**CONNECTION**

Increase Your Earning Power

Offering retail products to clients is important because a salon professional can earn an additional $3,000 to $5,000 a year through retail sales. It is typical for a successful professional to sell $40 per day in retail products. In addition, clients making purchases recommended by a professional tend to increase their trust in and develop a sense of loyalty to that professional.

DISCOVER**MORE**

A salon will only be successful if the clients are fully satisfied with their salon experience. Here are a few ways to find out what clients think about you, your salon and possibly even the competition:

Check the Web. More consumers are going to the Web and social media outlets to air their complaints and share their reviews. This can give you insight into the clients' thoughts about the strengths and weaknesses of your salon and possibly your skills and techniques as a professional.

Give them a call. Try to do this routinely, perhaps two or three times a year. Try to get clients to give you a short overview of how they feel about you, your salon and the services you have provided for them.

Have a chat. There is nothing better than taking the time to listen to your clients in person. Taking the time to talk to them will make sure they are satisfied with the salon experience and that they are comfortable within your salon.

Creating an exceptional experience can be accomplished with special attention to the details of the Service Essentials. Connecting builds rapport. Consulting works to analyze, visualize and organize the framework to move ahead with the service. Creating produces functionally and aesthetically pleasing results. Completing establishes the client's satisfaction and future follow-up.

LESSONS LEARNED

- To solidify your relationship with the client during the Complete Service Essential:
  - Reinforce client satisfaction
  - Make professional product recommendations
  - Prebook the client's next appointment
  - Complete client record card
  - End with a warm goodbye
  - Provide follow-up after the salon visit
- When recommending products and after-care advice, you should spell out the benefits of using the products by explaining what you used, why, and when and how the client should use it at home.

104^c GLOSSARY/INDEX

Abstract Level of Observation *9*
Gathering information from the basic and detail levels of observation to view the object in a more conceptual and less literal, concrete way (quantitative analysis).

Adapting As a Designer *28*
Composing and personalizing hair designs to meet your client's individual needs; one of the four cornerstones of design.

Alternation *21*
Design principle that is a sequential repetition in which two or more units occur in a repeating pattern; can break up the surface of an object and create interest.

Apple Body Shape *39*
Rounded shoulder line; average to big bust; fullness around the middle.

Asymmetrical Balance *22*
Off-center arrangement; created when weight is positioned unequally from a center axis.

Balance *22*
The state of equilibrium existing between contrasting, opposite or interacting elements; two types, symmetrical and asymmetrical.

Basic Level of Observation *9*
Observing the silhouette or three-dimensional form of an object.

Benefit *82*
Identifies what a product will do, such as: adds shine, reduces frizz, strengthens, protects and relaxes.

Body Types *36*
Body types fall into three main categories: ectomorph, mesomorph and endomorph.

Casual Style *52*
Clothing, hair and lifestyle choices based on comfort and/or low maintenance.

Celestial Axis *14*
Symbol used to identify straight and curved lines, angles and directions

Circle *11*
A closed, curved geometric shape with equal radii from a center point of origin.

Classic Style *52*
Traditional clothing, hair and lifestyle choices. They wear a coordinated wardrobe and classic colors such as navy, black, white, cream, beige, brown and gray.

Color *18*
Visual perception of the reflection of light.

Complete Service Essential *85*
Strategy used during a client consultation to review the service experience and client satisfaction, offer product recommendations, express appreciation and provide follow-up.

Concave Lines *13*
Lines that curve inward, like the inside of a sphere.

Concave Profile *47*
Side view of face with an inward curve, which is most often the result of a dominant, protruding forehead and chin or a small nose.

Connect Service Essential *62*
Strategy used during a client consultation to help establish rapport and build credibility with each client.

Consult Service Essential *69*
Strategy used during a client consultation to analyze client wants and needs, visualize the end result, organize the plan for follow-through and obtain client agreement.

Consultation *74*
A process that helps a professional understand exactly what clients expect from their visit to the salon.

Contrast *21*
Design principle in which a desirable relationship of opposites occurs; creates variety and stimulates interest within a design.

Convex Lines *13*
Lines that curve outward, like the outside of a sphere.

Convex Profile *47*
Side view of face with a strong or exaggerated outward curvature resulting from either a protruding nose or a sloping forehead or chin.

Cool Colors *18*
Colors that contain blue, green or violet; communicate a strong, edgy or confident quality.

Create Service Essential *76*
Strategy used during a client consultation to produce functional, predictable and pleasing results.

Creating As a Designer *24*
Practicing all aspects of hair design to build your expertise and performing hair design procedures with focus and precision to produce predictable results; one of the four cornerstones of design.

Crescent *11*
A curved shape that is a derivative of a circle.

Curvilinear *10*
Consists of curved lines.

Design *6*
Arrangement of shapes, lines and ornamental effects to create an artistic whole.

Design Elements *10*
Form, texture and color; major components of an art form, or a part of the artistic whole.

Design Principles *20*
Artistic arrangement patterns for the design elements to follow; repetition, alternation, progression and contrast.

Detail Level of Observation *9*
Observing the textures and/or color characteristics of an object, along with any ornamental effects (qualitative analysis).

Diagonal Lines *13*
Lines that fall between horizontal and vertical; energetic and imply motion

Diamond *11*
A shape consisting of two equal back-to-back triangles.

Diamond Face Shape *46*
Elongated and angular; its widest area is at the cheekbones, while the forehead and chin are narrow.

Dramatic Style *53*
Clothing, hair and lifestyle choices based on anything out of the ordinary; they want to draw attention and make heads turn.

Ectomorph *37*
A body type characterized by a tall and lanky, narrow frame.

Endomorph *37*
A body type characterized by a short, sturdy, soft and round frame.

Face Shape *42*
There are seven common face shapes: oval, round, square, oblong (rectangle), pear (trapezoid), diamond and heart (triangle).

Feature *82*
The characteristics of a product or "what's in it (a product)" such as: natural bristles, vitamin E and almond oil.

Form *10*
Three-dimensional representation of shape; consists of length, width and depth.

Gamine Style *53*
Clients are fashion-oriented and enjoy wearing the latest looks.

Half-Circle *11*
A derivative of a circle.

Heart (Triangle) Face Shape *46*
Long and angular; chin area is sometimes elongated and pointed, while forehead is wide.

Horizontal Line *13*
Parallel to the horizon or to the floor; give the impression of stability, weight and calmness.

Hourglass Body Shape *39*
Rounded bottom and thighs; small waist, full bust.

Inverted Triangle Body Shape *39*
Bottom half smaller than top; straight and squared shoulder line.

Kite *11*
A shape made up of two back-to-back unequal triangles.

Lifestyle *54*
Factors in a person's life such as job/career, hobbies, family, time willing to spend on hair, skill or ability to care for hair, and the money the client is willing to invest in hair maintenance.

Line *13*
Consists of a series of connected points.

Mesomorph *37*
A body type characterized by rectangle-shaped, athletic and muscular build.

Natural Style *52*
Wearing colors and materials that are found in nature; low-maintenance hair designs.

Neutral colors *18*
Not predominately warm or cool; include shades of brown, beige and gray; also known as "earth tones."

Oblong *11*
An elongated curvature shape with a closed end and an open end.

Oblong (Rectangle) Face Shape *45*
Long, narrow and angular; jawline is wide and almost horizontal.

Oval *11*
A closed, curved shape with unequal radii from a point of origin.

Oval Face Shape *44*
Rounded, long and narrow rather than wide and short; no dominant areas.

Pear (Trapezoid) Face Shape *45*
Most often elongated, with a forehead that is narrow and a jaw that is the widest area of the face.

Point *13*
A mark; when set into motion, becomes a line.

Profile *47*
Outline of an object from the side, especially the side view of the face and head.

Progression *21*
Design principle in which all units are similar yet gradually change proportionately in an ascending (increasing) or descending (decreasing) scale; leads the eye rhythmically within a design.

Proportion *8*
Relation of a part to its whole; e.g., the head of a woman should be $^1/_7$ of her overall body height, while the head of a man should be $^1/_8$ of his overall body height, is the standard proportion most artists consider ideal.

Qualitative Analysis *8*
Observing, naming and listing parts of an object.

Quantitative Analysis *8*
Determining the amount of each part of an object relative to size, proportion and dimension.

Rectangle *11*
A shape with two sets of parallel sides.

Rectangle Body Shape *39*
Narrow shoulders; small bust; non-defined waist; narrow hips.

Rectilinear *10*
Consisting of horizontal and vertical lines.

Repetition *20*
Design principle in which all units are identical except for position; creates a feeling of uniformity.

Romantic Style *53*
Clothing, hair and lifestyle choices are soft and feminine; silk, flower prints, lace, beads, and pastel shades of color.

Round Face Shape *44*
Looks circular; appears to be rather short and wide rather than long and narrow.

Seeing As a Designer *8*
Seeing as a designer means observing the world and objects around you and making connections using design elements and design principles; one of the four cornerstones of design.

Service Essentials *61*
Strategies used during the client consultation to ensure successful results; strategies include connect, consult, create and complete.

Shape *10*
Two-dimensional representation of form consisting of length and width.

Square *11*
A shape with four equal sides.

Square Face Shape *45*
Short and wide; looks angular with straight lines.

Straight Profile *47*
Side view of face with a very slight outward curvature from the front hairline to the tip of the nose, and from the tip of the nose to the chin.

Symmetrical Balance *22*
Created when weight is positioned equally on both sides of a center axis, creating a mirror image; also known as harmonious arrangement.

Texture *16*
The visual appearance or feel of a surface; two categories, unactivated (smooth), activated (rough).

Thinking As a Designer *8*
Refers to analyzing what you see, visualizing a new design and organizing a plan that will enable you to create that design; one of the four cornerstones of design.

Three Levels of Observation *9*
A system that designers use for studying, categorizing and communicating the reality around them in a common language; basic, detail and abstract.

Three-Sectioning *42*
Effective way to measure the proportions of the face; done by measuring the three sections of the face: section one is the front hairline to the middle of the eyebrows; section two is the middle of the eyebrows to the tip of the nose; section three is the tip of the nose to the tip of the chin.

Trapezoid *11*
A shape with two unequal parallel sides and two equal, nonparallel sides.

Triangle *11*
A geometric shape with three equal sides.

Triangle (Pear) Body Shape *39*
Full hips; defined waist; shoulders more narrow than hips; small top half.

Triangular *10*
Consists primarily of diagonal lines.

Vertical Line *13*
Perpendicular to the horizon or floor; implies strength, weightlessness or equilibrium.

Warm Colors *18*
Contain yellow, red or orange; give hair designs a passionate, energetic or exciting feel.

Preface 序

Timothy Light
黎天睦

I was very honored when Professor Wang Xiaojun asked me to write a preface to his excellent textbook. A highly successful teacher, an effective department administrator and leader, and a very accomplished scholar in applied linguistics and teaching materials, Professor Wang, as always, makes a significant contribution to the field with this much needed material. His natural gifts for leading are also evident, as he has been assisted in this project by five others. Anyone who has attempted to write a textbook with several other people knows the daunting challenges presented by the number. That the product has emerged so successfully is a credit to all of the participants.

I wish that there had been textbooks such as this one when I first began to study Chinese in the mid 1960's. Available to us in the United States at that time were oral texts for the beginning level that were based on grammar manipulation exercises and reading texts that were valued on the basis of the number of characters that one could learn in the shortest amount of time. Beyond the beginning level, classes in the United States tended not to branch too far beyond decoding and translation. (Not surprisingly,classes in Hong Kong and Taiwan were a good deal more interactive and demanding even then.) I also wish that there had been more widely available materials for studying Chinese for special purposes, such as a possible career in business.The Mandarin Center, the Taipei Language Institute, the Stanford Center (all in Taiwan) and the New Asia—Yale-in-China Chinese Language Centre at the Chinese University of Hong Kong all produced fine specially focused materials for use within their own walls.But American students studying at home were left largely in the dark that there were such things and so did not imagine there was a possibility of formally learning specialized vocabulary and discourse formats.

How far we have come is exemplified by ***A Business Trip to China—Conversation & Application.*** Notably interactive, these materials introduce vocabulary that is fundamental to business and provide useful and relevant dialogues and exercises to practice that vocabulary and the linguistic-cultural conventions for using that vocabulary in business situations. The authors have been imaginative and thoughtful in the situations which they have selected for the bases of the dialogues and accompanying exercises. They have been comprehensive in including practice with typical forms that business people must fill out during the course of their working day.

Going to a country to work when one has at one's command only a general knowledge of basic language is frequently quite disorienting. One can get along to a degree in the simplest of daily tasks and can negotiate transport and lodging and order a meal, but often even the most elementary tasks of one's professional life are simply out of reach. The fortunate students who study this book have before them the happy prospect of having a significant jump ahead of their predecessors when they arrive in China and begin to get to work.

The authors collectively—and especially Professor Wang are to be thanked for this contribution to the advancement of the students of Chinese.

To the Users

A Business Trip to China—Conversation and Application I and II are designed for learners at a preintermediate level who have learned basic Chinese in a variety of settings. They are English speakers, or are using English as their principal second language, and they are interested in having a career or doing business among Chinese speaking communities.

At the outset of the twenty-first century, Chinese is spoken by over 1.3 billion people— more than any other language. The demand for Chinese language instruction is therefore increasing rapidly. There is, however, a lack of suitable teaching materials for English speakers wanting to learn Chinese for business communication. Although some textbooks of business Chinese have recently been published in the U. S. and China, these materials tend to be designed for students who have studied Chinese for at least three years or more. Very often, the contents of these texts are quite complicated and use many uncommon business terms.

Students at overseas universities, with varying language backgrounds, often desire instruction in aspects of real world Chinese business language and culture. To provide a practical, motivating, and user-friendly business Chinese textbook, we have employed the following pedagogical approaches to meet the needs of both instructors and students:

■ A communicative approach: We believe that the fundamental goal of these textbooks is to improve learners' business Chinese communication abilities. For this purpose, the lessons in the textbooks feature a series of business conversations portraying a Western businessman's business trip to China. We have tried to make these conversations short and interesting in order to motivate students to "role play" and thus be able to memorize large portions of them. We have also carefully selected frequently used vocabulary words and terms; especially business vocabulary featured in the statistical sections, and "recycled" them throughout the conversations. In order to encourage students to speak using the target language without looking at the text, we have provided a series of pictures after each workbook lesson, thus encouraging students to speak out using the new vocabulary and sentence structures.

■ An integrated approach: To communicate with Chinese speakers in a business environment, not only are language skills required, but also a knowledge of Chinese business culture and economic information. Therefore, unlike most Chinese textbooks, we have included two components in addition to the textbook's language component —Chinese business culture and economic information. To introduce the culture in a more interesting and engaging way,

David— the American businessman who goes to China for the first time, narrates his own stories, including his personal experiences and culture shocks in the form of a diary. The "Economic Background" sections, included after each lesson, are introduced visually with concise tables and in plain English. We also believe that the four language skills—listening, speaking, reading and writing, are related to each other, even though they can be acquired at different paces. It is our goal to integrate the training of the four skills by designing a large number of exercises, many of which incorporate authentic materials.

■ An interactive approach: In order to provide a textbook that can meet most learners' needs, we have made the business Chinese easy enough for pre-intermediate students to get started, but also challenging enough to allow students of varying language experience to group together and learn from each other. Therefore, students will not have to wait to learn professional level language and usages until they reach an advanced level. In both the textbooks and workbooks, we have designed many communicative activities designed to foster interaction among students as well as between teachers and students. These activities include dialogues, questions and answers, group activities, and role-plays. We also believe that students should master basic sentence structures as well as generate new sentences while emphasizing communicative functions. In order to present grammatical training in a communicative manner, we have not only given concise explanations based on the features of each sentence structure, but also a basic format of the structure and examples of usage. In addition, we have provided substitutive drills as often as possible, and use or recycle the relevant vocabulary in those examples and drills.

In an effort to be user-friendly, this textbook series is divided into two parts (Ⅰ & Ⅱ), with each part having two volumes—a textbook and a workbook. According to a typical university curriculum, it will normally take one semester to cover each part of the course. Each lesson in the textbook includes two dialogues, grammar and sentence pattern drills, a diary in English comparing Chinese and Western business culture, concise economic information, and supplementary bilingual business words presented with statistical tables. Each dialogue is given in both simplified and traditional characters with the associated *Pinyin* and English translations. The workbooks are designed to complement the textbooks. For the students' convenience, each section in the workbook provides the vocabulary list for each dialogue appearing in the textbook. The various exercises (10 to 11 different kinds in each section) are based on communicative and interactive approaches with the focus on business conversation and applications. It is expected that instructors' preparation time will be saved while still meeting the various needs of students. The listening exercises should be used in conjunction with the accompanying CD. Appendices and bilingual vocabulary indices are also included in each book.

致使用者

础商务汉语——会话与应用》系列教材可供具有初级汉语水平以上的学习者使用。凡是以英语为母语或主要交流语言并有兴趣在中国及华人社区从事商务活动的人，都可使用本教材来提高商务汉语的交际能力。

在21世纪之初，以汉语为母语的人口已达到13亿，其数量超过了世界上其他任何一种语言。汉语热也迅速升温。但是，很多以英语为媒介语的学习者却难以找到适合他们使用的商务汉语教材。虽然这样的教材近年来在中国和国外都出版过一些，但是往往要求学习者具备三年以上的日常汉语训练后才能涉猎，其课文内容的冗长复杂和专业词汇的生僻晦涩常常使初学者望而生畏。国外高校的汉语学生尽管有着不同的语言文化背景，但是他们都渴求学习到中国商务活动中真实的语言和文化。为了给学习者提供一部实用方便而又生动有趣的入门教材，我们在教学法上进行了下列的探索和创新，以满足师生的需要。

■ 突出交际能力的训练：我们深信商务汉语教学基本的和最终的目的都是提高学习者在商务活动中的交际能力。因此，这套教材的课文内容跟随一位西方商人的中国之行一步步展开。与此同时，我们尽量使每课的对话简短真切而又生动有趣，以便鼓励学生进入角色，进而能够记住大部分内容。我们也在词频统计的基础上仔细地选取使用频率较高的词汇，尤其是商业词汇，并尽量增加这些高频词在对话和练习中的重现率。为了鼓励学生用学到的商务汉语自由进行交际，我们还在练习册每课的后面提供了连环图片，学习者可根据图片的情节线索尝试使用新学到的词语和句型。

■ 加强综合技能的培养：在中国或以华人为主的商务氛围中进行交流，不仅要求有汉语技能，同时也需要具备一定的商业文化知识和对当地经贸情况的了解。有鉴于此，本教材有别于大多数语言教材的地方是，除了语言这一要素之外，还添加了另外两个要素——中国的商业文化和经贸信息。为了使学习者对中国商务文化有身临其境的感受，美国商人大卫用日记体的形式分段扼要地讲述了他第一次到中国经商的切身体会和感悟到的文化差异。每课正文之后我们还采用图表和简明的英语介绍相关的商业信息。在语言方面，我们也强调综合能力的训练。我们认为，语言的听、说、读、写四种能力是相辅相成的，但不必同步发展。为此，我们设计并提供了大量的仿真练习以提高学习者综合的语言能力。

■ 提倡互动式教学:为了满足绝大多数学习者的需要,我们的教材一方面尽量化难为易,使具备初级汉语水平的学生就可开始学习商务汉语;另一方面则带有一定伸缩性和挑战性,以利于不同程度的学习者结成语言伙伴,互相学习,取长补短。这样,学生就可以根据自己的需要,早日选择学习的方向,而不必等到学完高年级日常汉语之后才接触职业汉语。在相互配合的课本和综合练习册中,我们设计了很多交际练习以鼓励学习者之间和师生之间的互动交流。这些活动包括对话、问答、分组活动、模拟角色等等。在突出交际能力训练的同时,我们也意识到学习者必须掌握基本句型及类推以生成新句子的能力。为了达到在商务交际活动中进行语法训练的目的,我们不仅根据每个句型的特点作了针对性的说明,而且提供了基本的句式和用例,并引导学生运用新学到的词语做大量的句型操练,以建立语言接受能力和生成能力的互动。

基于方便教学者使用的目的,本教材分为上下两册,每册包括课本和综合练习两个分册。根据比较常见的国外大学的课程安排,每册教材一般可供一个学期使用。课本中的每一课都包括两段对话、相关的句型、注释和替换练习,以及日记体的中外商务文化比较和简要的经贸信息。为了扩大学习者的词汇量且便于查阅参考,每课还有汉英对照的用图表分类列出的常用商务词汇。每段对话都有简体字、繁体字、汉语拼音和英文翻译的相互对照,以便于学习者根据自己的情况选择和参考。综合练习册配合课本的内容而设计。为了学习者的便利,练习册中每课都提供了与课文中每个对话对应的词汇表。为每课设计的各种不同的练习都以功能教学和互动教学理念为指导,注重商务汉语会话和商务汉语应用能力的训练。我们希望这些教学材料在满足学生需要的同时,也能够节省教师的备课时间。此外,每册教材还附有与课文和练习配套的CD 光盘,以及各类附录和双语词汇索引。

Abbreviations for Parts of Speech

Adj.	*Adjective*
Adv.	*Adverb*
AP	*Adjective Phrase*
AV	*Auxiliary Verb*
CE	*Common Expression*
Collo.	*Colloquial*
Conj.	*Conjunction*
Exc.	*Exclamation*
IE	*Idiomatic Expression*
Interj.	*Interjection*
Loc.	*Localizer*
MW	*Measure Word*
N	*Noun*
NP	*Noun Phrase*
Num.	*Numerals*
Obj.	*Object*
P	*Particle*
PN	*Proper Noun*
Pol.	*Polite Expression*
Prep.	*Preposition*
Pron.	*Pronoun*
PW	*Place Word*
QW	*Question Word*
Subj.	*Subject*
TW	*Time Word*
V	*Verb*
VP	*Verb Phrase*

Characters in the Story

人物介绍

大卫
David

玛丽
Mary

经理
manager

总裁
CEO

张小姐
Miss Zhang

厂长
factory director

第一课 到达
Lesson 1 Arrival

Dialogue 1 On the Airplane 在飞机上

一、在飞机上

空　姐：各位旅客，十分钟以后，我们就要到达北京首都机场了，请您系好安全带。

大　卫：终于到北京了，我真高兴！

李小姐：这是您第一次到中国吗？

大　卫：是的，我来北京做生意，这是我的名片，有事请跟我联系。

空　姐：北京到了，请您带好随身行李以及您的护照、签证和申报单，准备入关。

李小姐：要入关了，有人来接您吗？

大　卫：不知道，我们公司的秘书给中国公司发了电子邮件。希望有人来，要不然我就得坐出租汽车了。

李小姐：不用担心，这里“打的”很方便。

大　卫：打？打什么？我要坐车！

Pinyin

Duìhuà Ⅰ: Zài Fēijī Shang

Kōngjiě: Gè wèi lǚkè, shí fēnzhōng yǐhòu, wǒmen jiù yào dàodá Běijīng Shǒudū Jīchǎng le, qǐng nín jìhǎo ānquándài.

Dàwèi: Zhōngyú dào Běijīng le, wǒ zhēn gāoxìng!

Lǐ xiǎojie: Zhè shì nín dì-yī cì dào Zhōngguó ma?

Dàwèi: Shì de, wǒ lái Běijīng zuò shēngyi. Zhè shì wǒ de míngpiàn, yǒu shì qǐng gēn wǒ liánxì.

Kōngjiě: Běijīng dào le, qǐng nín dàihǎo suíshēn xíngli yǐjí nín de hùzhào、qiānzhèng hé shēnbàodān, zhǔnbèi rù guān.

Lǐ xiǎojie: Yào rù guān le, yǒu rén lái jiē nín ma?

Dàwèi: Bù zhīdào, wǒmen gōngsī de mìshū gěi Zhōngguó gōngsī fāle diànzǐ yóujiàn. Xīwàng yǒu rén lái, yàoburán wǒ jiù děi zuò chūzū qìchē le.

Lǐ xiǎojie: Búyòng dānxīn, zhèli “dǎ dī” hěn fāngbiàn .

Dàwèi: Dǎ? Dǎ shénme? Wǒ yào zuò chē!

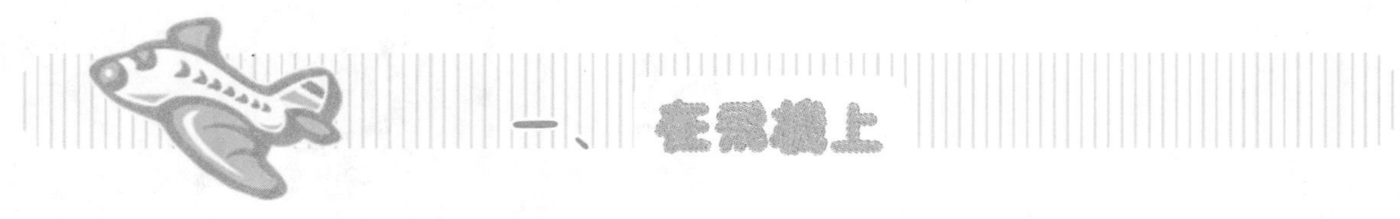

一、在飛機上

空　姐：各位旅客，十分鐘以後，我們就要到達北京首都機場了，請您繫好安全帶。

大　衛：終於到北京了，我真高興！

李小姐：這是您第一次到中國嗎？

大　衛：是的，我來北京做生意，這是我的名片，有事請跟我聯繫。

空　姐：北京到了，請您帶好隨身行李以及您的護照、簽证和申報單，準備入關。

李小姐：要入關了，有人來接您嗎？

大　衛：不知道，我們公司的秘書給中國公司發了電子郵件。希望有人來，要不然我就得坐出租汽車了。

李小姐：不用擔心，這裏“打的”很方便。

大　衛：打？打什麽？我要坐車！

ENGLISH TEXT

Dialogue Ⅰ: On the Airplane

Flight Attendant: Ladies and gentlemen, we will be arriving at Beijing Capital Airport in 10 minutes. Please fasten your seat belts.

David: I finally arrived in Beijing. I am so happy!

Miss Li: Is this your first time to come to China?

David: Yes, I've come to Beijing for business. Here is my business card for your future reference.

Flight Attendant: We have landed in Beijing. Please take your personal belongings and have your passport, visa and customs declaration form ready for arrival.

Miss Li: We are approaching customs. Do you have anyone to meet you?

David: I don't know. The secretary in our company sent an e-mail to the company in China. I hope someone will be here. Otherwise, I will have to take a taxi.

Miss Li: Do not worry. It is very convenient to "beat *Di*" here.

David: Beat? Beat what? I want to take a taxi!

Notes

Grammar & Pattern Drills

1. 在……上 (Prep. ...Loc.)

Location expressions include three parts：在 ＋ place ＋ localizer. Location expressions are used in the following positions：

(1) Before the verb, location expressions are used as a prepositional phrase to indicate location. Some of the most common localizers are "上，下，里，外，前面，后面，中间，旁边"。

Subj. ＋在＋place＋Loc. ＋V

Examples：

1. 老师在黑板上写字。

   The teacher is writing on the blackboard.

2. 孩子们在公园里玩。

   Children are playing in the park.

Substitutive drills:

小　王		飞机	上	看电视。
李小姐	在	机场	旁边	工作。
大　卫		汽车	里	休息。
空　姐		旅客	前面	讲话。

(2) Location expressions can also be placed after the verb to indicate a particular place.

Subj. ＋V＋在＋place ＋Loc.

Examples:

1. 我家住在城外。
   My family lives outside of town.
2. 医生站在护士旁边。
   The doctor is standing next to the nurse.

Substitutive drills:

名　片	放		桌子	上。
空　姐	坐	在	椅子	上。
王小姐	住		公司	里。
李先生	站		汽车	旁边。

2. 以后……就 (Loc. ...Adv.) "after... then"

以后 is placed at the end of a phrase or a time word , and 就 connects the action that takes place right after.

Examples:

1. 十分钟以后，商店就（要）关门了。

   10 minutes from now, the store is going to close.

2. 他吃完早饭以后，就去上班。

   After he finishes his breakfast, he will go to work.

Substitutive drills:

一个星期			工作		结束了。
十天			哥哥		要去中国了。
李小姐	到北京	以后，		就	去公司。
大卫有了	签证				去买飞机票。
我的朋友	吃完饭				发电子邮件。

3. 终于……了 (Adv. ...P) "finally"

The expression is used to describe a completion of an action after a long time or process.

ENGLISH TEXT

Dialogue Ⅱ: Going Through the Customs

David: I'm surprised! Beijing Airport is so huge!

Miss Li: Yes. Beijing has been developing very rapidly in recent years, and has become a modernized city.

David: Yes. By the way, do you know where I can get my luggage?

Miss Li: Look! The Baggage Claim Area is at the front. Do you have a lot of luggage?

David: No, not much, only two small pieces of luggage. I hope I won't have to wait too long.

Miss Li: It is OK to wait for a while. However, the custom inspectors are very strict. You didn't bring any illegal stuff, did you?

David: Illegal stuff? Of course not, I am a very conscientious foreigner. Look, I have already filled out my health statement form and arrival card.

Miss Li: Great! We can go claim our luggage together.

Notes

Grammar & Pattern Drills

1. 这么 (Adv.) "so"

这么 is followed by an adjective to emphasize the degree of an action or a fact.

Examples:

1. 出租汽车怎么这么慢!

   The taxi is so slow!

2. 时间过得这么快! 我们已经十年没见了。

   Time goes by so fast! We have not seen each other for ten years.

Substitutive drills:

你的行李	这么	多,	有人来接你吗?
公司		远,	我现在不想去。
大卫		聪明,	去中国做生意当然没有问题。
北京		大,	买东西一定很方便。

2. 可不是 (IE) "exactly"

可不是 is an informal agreement to respond to someone's opinion. It can also be said as 可不, 可不是吗.

Example:

A：检查人员挺严格。

The inspectors are very strict.

B：可不（是）！

Sure enough.

3. ……得＋AP （V ＋P ＋Complement）

Subj. ＋V＋得＋descriptive complement

Examples:

1. 她中文说得很快。

   She speaks Chinese very fast.

2. 这件事他办得很好。

   He handled this matter very well.

Substitutive drills:

李小姐行李	带	得	很多。
这个城市	发展		很快。
检查人员	检查		非常严。
他的入境卡	填		不清楚。

4. 挺…… (Adv.) "very, quite"

The meaning and usage of 挺 is similar to 很. However, 挺 is mostly used in spoken Chinese, and the degree of emphasis is not as strong as 很.

Examples:

1. 这件衣服挺好的，你应该买下来。

   This coat is quite good, you should buy it.

2. 这本书挺有意思。

   This book is quite interesting.

Substitutive drills:

你中文说得	挺	好的。
今天天气		热。
她的行李		多的。
这个飞机场		大的。

5. 什么 (Pron.) "any; some"

什么 refers to an indefinite thing, place, etc.

Examples:

1. 我想找个什么地方休息两天。

   I'm thinking of finding some place to rest for a couple of days.

2. 跟大卫做生意，没有什么不放心的。

   There is nothing to worry about when doing business with David.
3. 他没带什么行李。

   He doesn't have any luggage.
4. 他每天除了上课就没什么时间了。

   He has classes every day and has little free time left.

Substitutive drills:

我饿了，	想吃点儿	什么	东西。
开会时，	他没说		意见。
这次来，	他没买		礼物。
去医院检查	他没		病。

6. ……吧 (P)

(1) 吧 can be used at the end of a sentence to soften a request.

Examples:

1. 请进来吧！

   Please come in!
2. 我们回家吧！

   Let's go home!

Substitutive drills:

我们去中国	
我们一起做生意	吧!
快下飞机	

(2) 吧 can be added to the end of a statement to form a question implying surmise of supposition.

Examples:

1. 这个字你写错了吧?

   You wrote this character wrong, didn't you?

2. 你认识李先生吧?

   You know Mr. Li, don't you?

Substitutive drills:

你的护照和签证带了	
你的入境卡填好了	吧?
邀请函收到了	

出入国境的常用词语
Common Terms Used When Crossing the Border

表 2

English	Chinese	*Pinyin*
leave a country	出境	chū jìng
enter a country	入境	rù jìng
pass through the territory of a country	过境	guò jìng
passport	护照	hùzhào
visa	签证	qiānzhèng
identification card	身份证	shēnfènzhèng
customs	海关	hǎiguān
pass through the customs	入关	rù gān
declare sth. at the customs	报关	bào guān
customs inspection	海关检查	hǎiguān jiǎnchá
customs tariff	海关税则	hǎiguān shuìzé
declaration form	申报单	shēnbàodān
duty-free goods	免税商品	miǎnshuì shāngpǐn
passageway	通道	tōngdào
security check up	安检(安全检查)	ānjiǎn (ānquán jiǎnchá)
quarantine control	检疫	jiǎnyì
invitation letter	邀请函	yāoqǐnghán
entry or arrival card	入境卡	rùjìngkǎ
an import/export license	进/出口许可证	jìn/chūkǒu xǔkězhèng
health statement form	健康卡	jiànkāngkǎ

Introduction

Hi. My name is David. I have an MBA and spent the last several years working as a process improvement consultant. But I'm really an entrepreneur and have always wanted to start my own company——importing and exporting.

This book is about me and my first business trip to China. Included in each lesson is an entry from my journal, which I kept during my trip. Before going to China, I took a crash course in Mandarin and Chinese culture. Some of the things I encountered I anticipated, but others took me completely by surprise. My Chinese host was very helpful in answering my questions and helping me understand the protocol. As you read my journal and study Mandarin, I hope you will learn some things about Chinese business culture and also feel like "you are there".

WARNING: What you are about to read may induce unwanted culture shock. Symptoms include, but are not limited to, surprise, disbelief, gasps,and fits of laughter. Proceed at your own risk.

Day 1: Arrival

Business, Arrival and Health Cards

I arrived safe and sound in Beijing today. My flight was direct from Detroit and took about 14 hours. I made friends with a Chinese flight attendant and asked her many questions about China. She could speak both English and Mandarin fluently. We exchanged business cards (*ming-pian*) and I noticed she used both hands when giving me her card. She told me Chinese people pay great attention to titles on business cards.By knowing a person's position in his company, the Chinese know what level of respect to show.

Before landing, I had to complete an arrival card and health card (*jiankangka*). On the arrival card I had to disclose the purpose of my trip (business or pleasure) and where I would be staying during my visit. The health card is used as an attempt to prevent foreigners from bringing unwanted diseases into the country. The Chinese government is concerned about the spread of incurable diseases such as AIDS. I've heard public health education and facilities in China are not as sophisticated as they are in the West. I will soon see for myself.

Clearing Customs

The airport in Beijing is relatively new. I was surprised to see that it is quite large and modern. I'd say it ranks right up there with other airports in developed countries. Clearing customs was not difficult at all. I just needed to show my arrival card, health card and passport, including my 30-day visa. No one searched my luggage or hassled me.

Chinese Way of Honoring Guests

After clearing customs and getting my luggage, I was met by a small delegation of Chinese businessmen. Later, I realized one of them was our driver. They fussed over me like I was a celebrity. At first, this made me uncomfortable. Then I learned it is the Chinese way of honoring guests and showing friendship. Also, they did not tell me the itinerary or plan for the day. They like to take care of every detail and don't want their guests to worry about anything.

Book Chinese vs. Street Lingo

As soon as I got outside the airport, I quickly discovered the Mandarin I learned in class is quite different from what is spoken on the streets of Beijing. For example, I was called *Laowai*, which literally means "old foreigner". I found out this term is used for all foreigners regardless of their age. I also heard people asking about taxis, but they didn't use the term *chuzu qiche*, or "hired car" as I had learned. Instead, they called taking a taxi *da di*, which is a colloquial term used in Beijing.

Bargaining and Metered Taxis

My co-worker from America arrived later than me. He decided

to take a taxi from the airport to our hotel. After he got here, we discovered he paid too much for the taxi. Several taxi drivers at the airport approached him and he assumed they were all legitimate. However, our Chinese business partner told us that some of them are independent drivers. He told us to avoid them next time. He said they do not usually have meters and so you must bargain or pay their asking price. He told us to locate the taxi stand and only get in taxis that have meters. Meters can be seen on the dashboard and the price per kilometer is prominently displayed in the rear passenger window. The good news is he told us if we feel a taxi driver has cheated us, we can write down his ID number displayed with his photo on the dashboard and report it to the authorities. He said that sometimes just writing down a driver's number in plain view is enough to get him to adjust the fare. I'm glad I learned this lesson about taxis in China. I'm sure I will learn a lot more in the days to come.

General Introduction to the Chinese Economy

Enjoying an average of 7% ～9% economic growth per year since 1990, China was named one of the "Top 10 New Economic Power" by World Bank. According to statistics from the National Bureau of Statistics (NBS) of China, China's Gross Domestic Product (GDP) in 2004 reached RMB 13651. 5 billion *yuan*, ranking No.7 in the world. However, as the country with the largest population in the world, the per capita GDP of China in 2004 was only about 1240 US dollars, which placed it among middle-lower income countries.

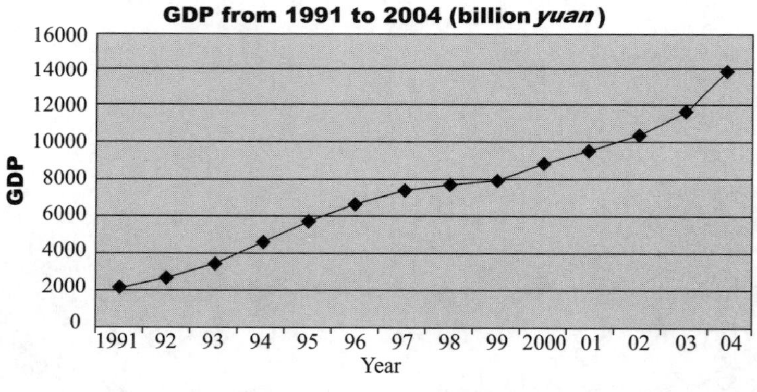

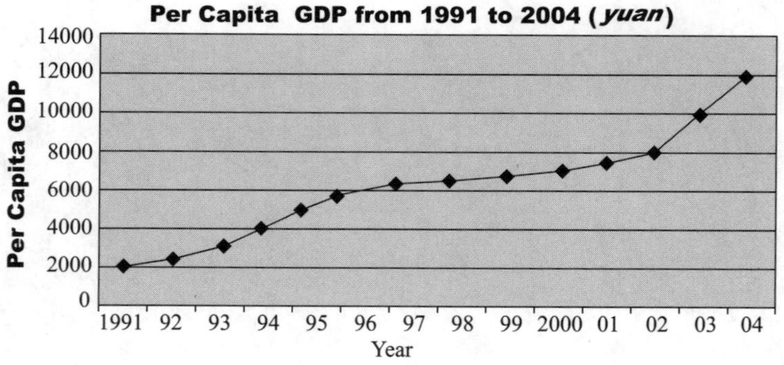

第二课 住宾馆

Lesson 2 Checking in at a Hotel

Dialogue 1 Registration 登记

一、登记

服务台：先生，请问，您要住宾馆吗？需要什么样的房间？

大　卫：单人房就行。一个晚上多少钱？

服务台：我们是四星级宾馆，档次比较高。一个晚上六百元人民币。

大　卫：需要先付押金吗？

服务台：不需要押金。但是我们需要看您的证件，并请您填写住房登记表。

大　卫：没有问题，这是我的护照和住房登记表。

服务台：谢谢。这是您的房间钥匙。您的房间号码是328，就在三楼右边，我们有人帮您拿行李。

大　卫：哦，对了，明天我要到银行办事儿，你可以叫我起床吗？

服务台：几点？

大　卫：早上七点，谢谢。

Pinyin

Duìhuà I：Dēngjì

Fúwùtái：Xiānsheng，qǐngwèn，nín yào zhù bīnguǎn ma? Xūyào shénmeyàng de fángjiān ?

Dàwèi：Dānrénfáng jiù xíng. Yí ge wǎnshang duōshao qián?

Fúwùtái：Wǒmen shì sìxīngjí bīnguǎn，dàngcì bǐjiào gāo，yí ge wǎnshang liùbǎi yuán rénmínbì.

Dàwèi：Xūyào xiān fù yājīn ma?

Fúwùtái：Bù xūyào yājīn，dànshì wǒmen xūyào kàn nín de zhèngjiàn，bìng qǐng nín tiánxiě zhùfáng dēngjìbiǎo.

Dàwèi：Méiyǒu wèntí. Zhè shì wǒ de hùzhào hé zhùfáng dēngjìbiǎo.

Fúwùtái：Xièxie. Zhè shì nín de fángjiān yàoshi. Nín de fángjiān hàomǎ shì sān-èr-bā，jiù zài sān lóu yòubian. Wǒmen yǒu rén bāng nín ná xíngli.

Dàwèi：Ò，duìle，míngtiān wǒ yào dào yínháng bàn shìr，nǐ kěyǐ jiào wǒ qǐ chuáng ma?

Fúwùtái：Jǐ diǎn?

Dàwèi：Zǎoshang qī diǎn，xièxie.

服務台：先生，請問，您要住賓館嗎？需要什麼樣的房間？

大　衛：單人房就行。一個晚上多少錢？

服務台：我們是四星級賓館，檔次比較高。一個晚上六百元人民幣。

大　衛：需要先付押金嗎？

服務台：不需要押金。但是我們需要看您的證件，並請您填寫住房登記表。

大　衛：没有問題，這是我的護照和住房登記表。

服務台：謝謝。這是您的房間鑰匙。您的房間號碼是328，就在三樓右邊，我們有人幫您拿行李。

大　衛：哦，對了，明天我要到銀行辦事兒，你可以叫我起床嗎？

服務台：幾點？

大　衛：早上七點，謝謝。

ENGLISH TEXT

Dialogue Ⅰ: Registration

Reception: Sir, would you like to check in? What kind of room do you need?

David: A single room will be fine. How much do you charge for a single room per night?

Reception: This is a high quality four-star hotel, so we charge six hundred RMB per night.

David: Do I need to pay a deposit first?

Reception: A deposit is not necessary, but we need to see your identification. Please fill out the hotel check-in form as well.

David: No problem. Here are my passport and check-in form.

Reception: Thank you. Here is your room key. Your room number is 328 and it is located on the right side of the third floor. We will have someone carry your luggage to your room.

David: Oh, by the way, I need to go to the bank to take care of some business tomorrow. Can you wake me up?

Reception: What time?

David: 7: 00 am. Thanks.

Grammar & Pattern Drills

1. ……就行 "... then it will be fine"

……就行 occurs at the end of the sentence, in neutral tones and a falling intonation, to indicate "it will be fine" or acceptable if that is the case.

Examples:

1. A：你想喝点儿什么？

   What do you want to drink?

   B：一杯水就行。

   Just one cup of water will be fine.

2. 我知道你很忙，有时间打个电话来就行。

   I know you are very busy. It will be fine if you can give me a call when you have time.

Substitutive drills:

我不喝咖啡，来杯水	
去旅行最好少拿东西，带上你的护照	
你到中国后给公司发一个电子邮件	就行。
你不用来飞机场接我，我打的	
我不需要五星级宾馆，有地方睡觉	

2. 需要 (AV/ V) "need; require"

需要 is the synonym of 要 in their common meaning of necessity. However, 要 has additional meanings, as illustrated in Lesson 1, to indicate "want" or something will happen, whereas 需要 does not has those usages. 需要 can be used as either an auxiliary verb or a verb.

(1) 需要 is followed by a verb or verb phrase when it is used as an auxiliary verb.

Examples:

1. 我需要去银行。

   I need to go to the bank.

2. 住宾馆需要填登记表。

   You are required to fill out the registration form to stay in a hotel.

(2) 需要 can be followed by a noun or noun phrase when it is used as a verb. It implies the need to get something.

3. 我需要一间单人房。

   I need a single room.

Substitutive drills:

入关时		填写申报单。
你		去机场接你吗?
我们	需要	坐出租车去宾馆。
服务台小姐		看您的证件。
明天李先生		去银行办事。

3. 一(个)……多少钱 (unit ＋quantifier) "how much per unit"

This pattern is used to compute the quantity or frequency of an action per unit as a standard of measurement. It has two parts. The first part is the unit that the computation is based on, and the second part indicates the quantity or frequency of an action based on each unit.

Examples:

1. 飞机票一张五百美元。
   It costs US$500 for one airplane ticket.
2. 她经常出国，一个月两次。
   She often goes abroad, twice a month.

Substitutive drills:

	一张从纽约到上海的飞机票	
	单人房一个月	
请问，	坐出租车十公里	多少钱？
	北京的五星级宾馆一天	
	打长途电话一分钟	

4. 先 (Adv.) "first; in advance"

先 is usually used before a verb or verb phrase to indicate "first" or "doing something before something else".

Examples:

1. 租房子要先付押金。

   You have to pay the deposit in advance in order to rent a house.

2. 明天上午我要先给公司打个电话。

   I will call the company first tomorrow morning.

Substitutive drills:

明天我要		去银行。
下飞机后我		去领行李。
我	先	来介绍一下。
下飞机前请		填好申报表。
请你		给公司的秘书发个电子邮件。

5. 有＋sb.＋VP *Pivot sentence*

"Sb." here is the object of the first verb 有，it is also the subject of the following verb phrase. Consider the following two sentences：

A. Our company has a person.

B. This person can help you carry your luggage.

In Chinese, we can combine these two sentences into one by "pivoting" on "this person" and the sentence means "our company has someone who can help you carry your luggage".（我们公司有人帮你拿行李。）

Examples:

1. 我们公司有人在中国做生意。

   Our company has people who are doing business in China.

2. 她有朋友在机场工作。

   She has a friend who works at the airport.

Substitutive drills:

美国公司		人	来机场接我。
大卫		朋友	在中国工作。
李先生	有	个女儿	在美国做生意。
中国		很多学生	在美国读书。
宾馆里		人	帮旅客拿行李。

6. 对了 (Interj.) "by the way"

对了 literally means "that is correct". It can also be used as an interjection during the conversation, depending on the context, to mean "by the way".

Examples:

1. 我明天要去中国。对了，中国公司有人来机场接我吗？

   I will go to China tomorrow, By the way, is there someone from the Chinese company who will pick me up at the airport?

2. 认识你很高兴。对了，这是我的名片。

   Nice to meet you . By the way , this is my business card.

Substitutive drills:

请打电话给我。	对了，	这是我的名片。
我要一间单人房。		需要先付押金吗?
我下飞机后得坐出租车。		北京的出租车贵不贵?
您的房间号是 524。		这是房间钥匙。

7. 可以 (AV) "can"

可以 can be replaced by 能 with the meaning of possibility. However, 可以 has an additional meaning of "be permitted", whereas 能 mainly indicates "ability" or "capability".

Examples:

1. 你可以在宾馆等我吗?

   Can you possibly wait for me at the hotel?

2. 你可以带一件随身行李上飞机。

   You are permitted to carry one piece of luggage with you when you board the airplane.

Substitutive drills:

你		在上海工作一年吗？
在中国	可以	用电子邮件订房间吗？
飞机上不		抽烟。
我们公司		去飞机场接你们。

中国旅馆的常用名称
Common Names used for Chinese Hotels

表 3

English	Chinese	*Pinyin*	Usage
hotel; restaurant	饭店	fàndiàn	higher grade
hotel; guesthouse	宾馆	bīnguǎn	higher grade
inn; hotel	旅馆/旅店	lǚguǎn / lǚdiàn	ordinary hotel
motel	汽车旅馆	qìchē lǚguǎn	
hostel	招待所	zhāodàisuǒ	a building with simple accommodation
reception center	接待中心	jiēdài zhōngxīn	hosting guests for conferences,exhibitions, etc.

中国宾馆的各类设施
Various Facilities in Chinese Hotels

表 4

English	Chinese	*Pinyin*
assembly hall	大礼堂/大厅	dàlǐtáng / dàtīng
banquet hall	宴会厅	yànhuìtīng
Chinese food restaurant	中餐厅	zhōngcāntīng
Western food restaurant	西餐厅	xīcāntīng
buffet restaurant	自助餐厅	zìzhù cāntīng
gymnasium; gym	健身房	jiànshēnfáng
conference room	会议室	huìyìshì
song and dance hall	歌舞厅	gēwǔtīng
entertainment hall	娱乐厅	yúlètīng
bar; pub	酒吧	jiǔbā
coffee house; café	咖啡厅	kāfēitīng
health center	保健中心	bǎojiàn zhōngxīn
business center	商务中心	shāngwù zhōngxīn
service desk	服务台	fúwùtái
security section	保安室	bǎo'ānshì
restroom	洗手间/厕所	xǐshǒujiān / cèsuǒ
separate room (in a restaurant); chartered room	包间	bāojiān

北京饭店
BEIJING HOTEL

Dialogue 2 Services

服 务

二、服务

(大卫房间的空调坏了，他给服务台打电话。)

服务台：服务台。先生，有事吗？

大　卫：这个房间的空调好像坏了，请帮忙检查一下。

服务台：好，工作人员马上就去。

大　卫：请问，房间里的保险箱怎么用？

服务台：先付押金，再自选密码。您随身带的贵重物品也可以交服务台保管。

大　卫：那太好了。还有，在宾馆可以发传真吗？

服务台：可以，我们的商务中心不但有传真服务，而且有复印机，还可以上网。

大　卫：在房间里可以用手提电脑吗？

服务台：对不起，房间里还没有联网，但是你可以在网吧里收发电子邮件。

大　卫：那怎么结账呢？贵不贵？

服务台：不贵，要是你没带现金，也可以用信用卡结账。

大　卫：麻烦您了。可是，我还没有申请中国的信用卡呢！

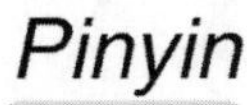

Pinyin

Duìhuà II: Fúwù

(Dàwèi fángjiān de kōngtiáo huài le, tā gěi fúwùtái dǎ diànhuà.)

Fúwùtái: Fúwùtái. Xiānsheng, yǒu shì ma?

Dàwèi: Zhè ge fángjiān de kōngtiáo hǎoxiàng huài le, qǐng bāngmáng jiǎnchá yíxià.

Fúwùtái: Hǎo, gōngzuò rényuán mǎshàng jiù qù.

Dàwèi: Qǐngwèn, fángjiān li de bǎoxiǎnxiāng zěnme yòng?

Fúwùtái: Xiān fù yājīn, zài zìxuǎn mìmǎ. Nín suíshēn dài de guìzhòng wùpǐn yě kěyǐ jiāo fúwùtái bǎoguǎn.

Dàwèi: Nà tài hǎo le. Háiyǒu, zài bīnguǎn kěyǐ fā chuánzhēn ma?

Fúwùtái: Kěyǐ, wǒmen de shāngwù zhōngxīn búdàn yǒu chuánzhēn fúwù, érqiě yǒu fùyìnjī, hái kěyǐ shàng wǎng.

Dàwèi: Zài fángjiān li kěyǐ yòng shǒutí diànnǎo ma?

Fúwùtái: Duìbuqǐ, fángjiān li hái méiyou liánwǎng, dànshì nǐ kěyǐ zài wǎngbā li shōu fā diànzǐ yóujiàn.

Dàwèi: Nà zěnme jié zhàng ne? Guì bu guì?

Fúwùtái: Bú guì, yàoshi nǐ méi dài xiànjīn, yě kěyǐ yòng xìnyòngkǎ jié zhàng.

Dàwèi: Máfan nín le. Kěshì, wǒ hái méiyou shēnqǐng Zhōngguó de xìnyòngkǎ ne!

二、服務

(大衛房間的空調壞了，他給服務台打電話。)

服務台：服務台。先生，有事嗎？

大　衛：這個房間的空調好像壞了，請幫忙檢查一下。

服務台：好，工作人員馬上就去。

大　衛：請問，房間裏的保險箱怎麼用？

服務台：先付押金，再自選密碼。您隨身帶的貴重物品也可以交服務台保管。

大　衛：那太好了。還有，在賓館可以發傳真嗎？

服務台：可以，我們的商務中心不但有傳真服務，而且有複印機，還可以上網。

大　衛：在房間里可以用手提電腦嗎？

服務台：對不起，房間裏還沒有聯網，但是你可以在網吧裏收發電子郵件。

大　衛：那怎麼結賬呢？貴不貴？

服務台：不貴，要是你沒帶現金，也可以用信用卡結賬。

大　衛：麻煩您了。可是，我還沒有申請中國的信用卡呢！

ENGLISH TEXT

Dialogue Ⅱ: Services

(David found out the air conditioner was not working in his room, so he called the reception desk.)

Reception: Front desk. Sir, how can I help you?

David: The air conditioner in my room doesn't seem to be working. Can you please help me out and inspect it?

Reception: Sure, our maintance man will be right over.

David: May I ask how to use the safe in the room?

Reception: Please pay the deposit first and then select your own password. Your personal valuables can be stored at the reception desk as well.

David: That is great. Also, can I send a fax in the hotel?

Reception: Yes. Our business center provides fax service as well as a copy machine. You can also get on the Internet.

David: Can I use my laptop in my room?

Reception: Sorry, our guest rooms do not have Internet connections yet, but you can read your e-mail at the Internet café.

David: How do I pay for the service? Is it expensive?

Reception: No, not expensive at all. If you do not have cash with you, you can pay with a credit card.

David: Thank you for your assistance. I haven't, however, applied for a Chinese credit card yet.

Notes

Grammar & Pattern Drills

1. 好像……(似的/一样) (Adv.) "seem; be like"

好像 can be placed either before the verb phrase or the subject. 似的 or 一样 can be added to the end of the sentence. Sometimes, 好像 can be replaced by 好像是.

Examples:

1. 他常常去北京，好像他的家在北京似的。
   He often goes to Beijing. It seems that his home is in Beijing.
2. 李先生明天早上五点就要起床，好像很忙。
   Mr. Li will get up at 5 o'clock tomorrow morning. He seems very busy.

Substitutive drills:

李先生		还没有填写申报单	
中国的上海		美国的纽约	
大卫到了北京	好像	回家了	(似的)。
李小姐		是大卫的老朋友	
这个美国人中文说得		中国人	

2. 先(Adv.)……再(Adv.)……然后(Conj.)…… "first...then...after that..."

先……再 or 先……然后 or 先……再……然后 can be used as a group of adverbs to connect two or more events or actions in sequence, and they can be used either in the past or the future tense. Note that 先 or 再, as an adverb, can't be placed before the subject.

Examples:

1. 我先去北京，然后去台北。
   I will go to Beijing first, then go to Taipei.
2. 请你先取行李，再出关，然后我们打的去宾馆。
   Please pick up your luggage first, then we will go to the hotel by taxi after you pass through the customs.

Substitutive drills:

大卫		下飞机，		去取行李，		入关。
请您	先	到东京，	再	去北京，	然后	飞上海。
李小姐		填住房登记表，		付押金，		去她房间。

3. Clause/VP＋的＋NP "*Clause/VP*" *as a modifier*

In Chinese, a clause or verb phrase may be placed before a noun to serve as a modifier of the noun with 的 in between. The clause or verb phrase embedded in a noun phrase functions as a relative clause in English.

Consider the following two sentences:

①I like this shirt.

我喜欢这件衬衫。

②My mother bought this shirt for me in Taipei.

我妈妈给我在台北买了这件衬衫。

In English, we can combine the two sentences into one, and use the second sentence as a relative clause, i. e.

③I like this shirt that my mother bought for me in Taipei.

In Chinese, the relative clause is placed at the beginning of the noun phrase and is followed by the modifier marker 的, as in the following example:

④我喜欢妈妈在台北给我买的这件衬衫。

The noun phrase with a clause or a VP as the modifier can be used as either a subject or an object in a sentence.

Examples:

1. 在上海做生意的李先生是我的好朋友。

   Mr. Li, who is doing business in Shanghai, is my good friend.

2. 您填写的登记表请交给服务台。

   Please turn in the registration form that you have filled out to the service desk.

Substitutive drills:

我喜欢住	公司介绍	的	那个宾馆。
李小姐认识了	在北京工作		那位先生。

住在 328 房间	的	那个美国人	是我的朋友。
去机场接你		那位小姐	是我们公司的秘书。

4. 还有 (Conj.) "still more; moreover"

还有 can be used independently as a conjunction phrase to add in a new topic after the one before. It can also be used to add another thing or item.

Examples:

1. 明天公司的秘书要去银行。还有，大卫要去机场。
   The company secretary will go to the bank tomorrow. Also, David will go to the airport.
2. 服务台，请明天早上六点叫我起床，还有，可以帮我发一份传真吗?
   Service desk, please wake me up at 6:00 tomorrow morning. Also, can you help me send a fax?

The other usage of 还有 is to mean "also have". 还有 is used as a verb phrase.

3. 我的名片上有中文，还有英文。
   There is both Chinese and English on my business card.

Substitutive drills:

大卫想去中国做生意。	还有，	他也想在中国学习中文。
请带好您的护照。		您的名片。
入关时请填好申报单。		健康卡。
这家宾馆有传真服务。		在房间里可以用手提电脑。

5. 不但……而且…… (Conj.) "not only... but also..."

The usage of 不但……而且…… is to connect two related clauses. 不但 usually precedes the second clause containing 而且. 而且 expresses the meaning of "furthermore". If two clauses share the same subject, 不但 is usually placed after the subject; if each clause has a different subject, 不但 is normally placed before the subject.

Examples:

1. 她不但是李先生的秘书，而且是李先生的朋友。
   Not only is she Mr. Li's secretary, but also his friend.
2. 不但王先生在中国做生意，而且王太太也常去中国做生意。
   Not only is Mr. Wang doing business in China, Mrs. Wang also often goes to China to do business.

不但……而且……can also connect two noun phrases or prepositional phrases, but both phrases must be placed before the predicate.

3. 不但中国人，而且很多外国人都喜欢吃饺子。

   Both Chinese and many foreigners like *jiaozi*.

4. 我们公司不但在国内，而且在国际上都很有名。

   Our company is well-known not only in China, but also internationally.

Substitutive drills:

他今天上午		要去银行，		还要开会。
大卫		在北京，		在台北做生意。
李小姐	不但	会说北京话，	而且	也会说英文。
北京首都机场		大，		很方便。
住这家宾馆的		有中国人，		有很多外国人。

6. 要是……（的话） (Conj.) "if; in case"

要是 is a conjunction word that is usually placed in the first clause, either before or after the subject, to express an assumption. It is optional to add 的话 to the end of the phrase.

Examples:

1. 要是没有带手提电脑，你可以去网吧收发电子邮件。

   If you didn't bring your laptop computer, you may go to the Internet café to receive and send e-mails.

2. 要是李小姐有时间的话，请她帮我复印。

   Please ask Miss Li to help me make copies if she has time.

   Sometimes，要是 can be followed by noun only.

3. 要是我，就不住宾馆了。

   If it were me，I wouldn't stay in a hotel.

4. 要是去年，检查人员就不会这么严格了。

   The security officers wouldn't be so strict if this were last year.

Substitutive drills：

要是	你不会中文	（的话），	李小姐可以帮你填写。
	你有贵重物品		服务台可以存放。
	在美国		大卫就不用打的。
	我会英文		就到美国去做生意。

7. 还……（呢） (Adv.) "still；yet"

还 is usually placed after the subject of a sentence and before a verb phrase to mean a situation or an action is still going on. 呢 associated with 还，is usually placed at the end of the sentence to emphasize the fact.

Examples：

1. 已经两个小时了，可是他还没有上飞机。

   It has already been two hours，but he hasn't boarded the airplane yet.

2. 一个晚上她好像都没有睡觉。现在她还在上网呢。
It seems that she didn't go to sleep the whole night. Right now she is still on the Internet.

Substitutive drills:

晚上十一点了，大卫	还	没有吃晚饭	（呢）。
李小姐		没有去过美国	
她在中国工作一年了，		没有学会中文	
王先生		在用电脑	

中国邮政通讯服务常用词语
Common Terms of Postal/Communication Services

表 5

English	Chinese	*Pinyin*
ordinary mail	平信	píngxìn
registered mail	挂号信	guàhàoxìn
express mail (package)	快件	kuàijiàn
package; parcel	包裹	bāoguǒ
postage	寄费/邮费	jìfèi / yóufèi
stamp	邮票	yóupiào
e-mail	电子邮件	diànzǐ yóujiàn
fax	传真	chuánzhēn
electronic transfer	电汇	diànhuì
public phone	公用电话	gōngyòng diànhuà
local call	市内电话	shìnèi diànhuà
long distance call	长途电话	chángtú diànhuà
telephone directory	电话簿	diànhuàbù
calling card	电话卡	diànhuàkǎ
telephone	座机	zuòjī
cell phone	手机	shǒujī
walkie-talkie	对讲机	duìjiǎngjī
text message	手机短信	shǒujī duǎnxìn
Internet	因特网	yīntèwǎng
web-site	网站	wǎngzhàn
log onto the Internet	上网	shàng wǎng

Later on Day 1: Checking into a hotel

Check-in, Porters and Tipping

When I arrived at my hotel, a porter opened the door for me. At the front desk, I had to show my passport and complete certain paperwork since I'm a foreigner. I was glad I could use my credit card to pay for the room. My host told me most Chinese still use cash. After I got my key, another porter carried my luggage to my room. My host told me to be sure to tip him two or three *kuai.* Later, at dinner, I learned it is not customary to tip waiters or waitresses.

How Many Stars?

The place where I'm staying——the Great Wall Sheraton——is close to downtown and rated four stars. In China, that's almost the best. Only a five star rating is better. Four star hotels in China are similar to expensive hotels in New York, Chicago or any other big city in America and can cost anywhere from $250 to $400 per night. However, my Chinese host thinks Americans would be happy staying in a two or three star hotel if it's in a major city like Beijing. Except for being out of the way, two and three star hotels have air conditioning, 24-hour hot water and many other "standards" that Americans are used to, but only cost between $30 and $60 per night.

Service and Security

One difference I see between American and Chinese hotels relates to service. Hotels I'm used to in America are basically self-serve. In other words, service is only provided upon request. Many do not have full-service restaurants. In China, I'm learning that most hotels have several restaurants. Service is considered important and automatically provided. My hotel offers more personal services than hotels in the USA, but everything costs extra.

My hotel caters to foreigners, so they have an exercise room. Most Chinese hotels do not have weight rooms or exercise facilities, although they are becoming more popular, but many have a pool and steam/sauna room with massage services. I've been told these massage services are non-sexual and should be considered safe.

So far I feel pretty safe. My room has a safe where I am storing my passport, camera and cash. However, since China is a group-oriented society, privacy has a different meaning than it does in America. As an example, hotel employees enter my room whenever they want. It's all in the name of service. They want to make sure I'm comfortable and have everything I need. Tomorrow, I will put the DO NOT DISTURB sign on the door. (It doesn't always work though.)

Internet, Faxing and E-mail

Before going to bed, I wanted to check my e-mail so I went to the lobby to ask if they had Internet access. A staff person took me to the hotel's business center. She showed me how I could send and receive faxes at a cost of 20 *yuan* per page——and check e-mail via the Internet at a cost of 40 *yuan* per hour. I thought it was a little pricey, and when I complained, she told me there are many Internet cafés within walking distance from the hotel. She said they charge anywhere from 4 to 10 *yuan* per hour, but the computers may not have English operating systems and may be slow. I have my laptop with me. I think my host told me I could use a public Internet service provider in Beijing using access codes 163 or 263 from the phone in my room, but I didn't get all the details.

Chinese Hotels

More than 5,200 star-rated hotels in China accommodate foreign visitors, with a total of 816 thousand guest rooms and 1.5 million beds. All these hotels are rated according to established international star-rating standards and accommodate foreign visitors. Familiar chains such as Sheraton, Holiday Inn, Hyatt, Hilton, and Ramada now operate deluxe hotels throughout China. A hotel rated with three or more stars have complete business centers with computer and secretarial services available, offering many other services such as foreign exchange conversion, flight arrangement, as well as facilities according to international standards. They also have English-speaking staff to deal with the foreign guests. The guest can ask for reception if they need.

All Chinese hotels open to foreigners receive reservations around-the-clock. People can make reservations via telephone at home or via other means such as fax, telex, telegram or on-line reservation. People usually check-in at noon and check out at 2:00 pm.

To help foreign tourists better understand traditional Chinese culture, there are also some hotels in Beijing like International Youth Hostel, known for its traditional Beijing features. The hostel is converted *siheyuan* (a compound with houses around a courtyard) deep in a long, narrow *hutong* (back-street lane). It is surrounded by the famous *Liulichang* Street and a Guildhall of Hubei and Hunan Provinces (also known as the Beijing Museum of Traditional Opera). It also organizes such activities as watching Beijing Opera, drinking at teahouses, and hiking along the Great Wall. People who stay here can have a real taste of traditional Chinese life.

第三课 银行
Lesson 3 Banking

Dialogue 1 Would You Like to Open an Account?

您要开户吗？

一、您要开户吗？

营业员：先生，您好。

大　卫：我想开一个账户。

营业员：没问题。您想要开什么样的账户？我们有两种：活期和定期。

大　卫：有支票账户吗？

营业员：对不起，我们没有支票账户。

大　卫：那么我开一个活期和一个定期。你们的利率是多少？

营业员：活期的利率很低。定期的年利率是百分之五。每个月利息会自动转到您的账户里。

大　卫：我可以申请提款卡和信用卡吗？

营业员：当然可以。请您填写这些表格，我就可以帮您开户，办理提款卡和信用卡。

大　卫：你们提供电汇和贷款的服务吗？

营业员：当然，请您上二楼的汇款部，有专人帮您办理。

Pinyin

Duìhuà I：Nín Yào Kāi Hù ma?

Yíngyèyuán： Xiānsheng，nín hǎo.

Dàwèi： Wǒ xiǎng kāi yí ge zhànghù.

Yíngyèyuán： Méi wèntí. Nín xiǎng yào kāi shénmeyàng de zhànghù? Wǒmen yǒu liǎng zhǒng：huóqī hé dìngqī.

Dàwèi： Yǒu zhīpiào zhànghù ma?

Yíngyèyuán： Duìbuqǐ，wǒmen méiyǒu zhīpiào zhànghù.

Dàwèi： Nàme wǒ kāi yí ge huóqī hé yí ge dìngqī. Nǐmen de lìlǜ shì duōshao?

Yíngyèyuán： Huóqī de lìlǜ hěn dī. Dìngqī de niánlìlǜ shì bǎi fēn zhī wǔ. Měi ge yuè lìxī huì zìdòng zhuǎndào nín de zhànghù li.

Dàwèi： Wǒ kěyǐ shēnqǐng tíkuǎnkǎ hé xìnyòngkǎ ma?

Yíngyèyuán： Dāngrán kěyǐ. Qǐng nín tiánxiě zhèxiē biǎogé，wǒ jiù kěyǐ bāng nín kāi hù，bànlǐ tíkuǎnkǎ hé xìnyòngkǎ.

Dàwèi： Nǐmen tígōng diànhuì hé dàikuǎn de fúwù ma?

Yíngyèyuán： Dāngrán，qǐng nín shàng èr lóu de huìkuǎnbù，yǒu zhuānrén bāng nín bànlǐ.

一、您要開户嗎？

營業員：先生，您好。

大　衛：我想開一個賬户。

營業員：沒問題。您想要開什麼樣的賬户？我們有兩種：活期和定期。

大　衛：有支票賬户嗎？

營業員：對不起，我們沒有支票賬户。

大　衛：那麼我開一個活期和一個定期。你們的利率是多少？

營業員：活期的利率很低。定期的年利率是百分之五。每個月利息會自動轉到您的賬户裏。

大　衛：我可以申請提款卡和信用卡嗎？

營業員：當然可以。請您填寫這些表格，我就可以幫您開户，辦理提款卡和信用卡。

大　衛：你們提供電匯和貸款的服務嗎？

營業員：當然，請您上二樓的匯款部，有專人幫您辦理。

ENGLISH TEXT

Dialogue Ⅰ: Would You Like to Open an Account?

Teller: How are you, Sir?

David: I would like to open an account.

Teller: No problem. What kind of account do you have in mind? We have two kinds of accounts: current and CD.

David: Do you have checking account?

Teller: Sorry, we do not have checking account.

David: Then I will open one current account and one CD account. What is your rate?

Teller: The interest for current account is very low. The APR for CDs is 5%. The interest will automatically be added to your account monthly.

David: Can I apply for an ATM card and a credit card?

Teller: Sure, please fill out these forms. Then I will be able to help you open the account and apply for a debit card and credit card.

David: Do you provide electronic wire transfer and loan services?

Teller: Of course. Please go to the Transaction Unit on the second floor. Someone will help you take care of the related matters.

Notes

Grammar & Pattern Drills

1. 想(V/Auxil. V)＋VP "would like to, want"

想 is placed before other verbs to express wishes or desires.

Examples:

1. 我想喝一杯可乐。
   I would like to drink a glass of cola.
2. 他想去图书馆看书。
   He would like to read books in the library.

Substitutive drills:

爸爸		在中国银行开账户。
他们	想	一起学中文。
我		做生意，顺便旅行。
我们		去银行申请信用卡。

2. 那么 (Conj.) "then"

那么 can function as a cohesive device in a dialogue to join a clause that indicates the result or judgement.

Example:

A：今晚我们去跳舞，怎么样？

Let's go dancing tonight. How does that sound?

B：我今天很累，不想去跳舞。

I'm very tired today. I don't feel like going dancing.

A：那么我们就在家看电视吧。

Then we can just stay home and watch TV.

Substitutive drills:

A:		B:
我没有人民币了。	那么	我们去银行吧。
这几年中国发展得很快。		我们去中国做生意。
我的电脑坏了。		你给我发传真吧。
大卫还没在中国银行开账户。		请他快去申请。

3. 百分之…… (numeric phrase) "...percent"

百分之……is a fixed form to show percent in Chinese. It is equivalent to "%". 百分比 is used as a noun phrase meaning percentage. 百分之百 can be used as an adjective to indicate "absolutely", "one hundred-percent".

Examples:

1. 今天定期存款的年利率是百分之三。

   The interest rate for one year CD is 3% today.

2. 活期账户的利率是百分之几?

What is the interest rate for the current account?

Substitutive drills:

这家宾馆的客房出租率是	百分之	六十。
请问，买车贷款的年利率是		几?
在这家银行开账户是		百的保险。

4. 帮 (V) "to help"

帮，a transitive verb, can have a direct object, such as 请你帮我. In this lesson, it is followed by a "pivotal" object to express "help someone do something".

Subj. ＋帮＋Obj. ＋V

Examples:

1. 他帮我拿行李。

   He helped me carry the luggage.

2. 我帮妈妈打扫房子。

   I helped my mother clean up the house.

Substitutive drills:

姐姐		妈妈	做晚饭。
我		同学	拿书。
李小姐	帮	客人	发传真。
营业员		史先生	开账户。
秘书		大卫	印名片。

中国常用的"卡"
Cards Commonly Used in China

表 6

English	Chinese	*Pinyin*
credit card	信用卡	xìnyòngkǎ
debit card	提款卡	tíkuǎnkǎ
bank card	银行卡	yínhángkǎ
discount / favourable card	优惠卡	yōuhuìkǎ
membership card	会员卡	huìyuánkǎ
quality certificate	质量卡	zhìliàngkǎ
guarantee card	保修卡	bǎoxiūkǎ

中国工商
自动柜员机
中国工商
自动柜员机
商品除外

Dialogue 2 Currency Exchange

美元换人民币

二、美元换人民币

玛　丽：我想要用美元兑换人民币。

营业员：好的，请到那边的柜台填表格。这是今天的牌价。

玛　丽：今天的兑换率还不错。

营业员：请问，您要用现金还是旅行支票兑换人民币？

玛　丽：用现金。

营业员：要换多少钱？

玛　丽：两百美元。你们除了美元，还收其他货币吗？

营业员：我们也收英镑、欧元、日元和港币、新台币。

玛　丽：太好了。怎么办理手续？

营业员：请您填一下兑换表格。

玛　丽：我还有一些美元想存在银行，你们有外汇存款吗？

营业员：有，我们银行提供全方位的服务。

Pinyin

Duìhuà II : Měiyuán Huàn Rénmínbì

Mǎlì: Wǒ xiǎng yào yòng měiyuán duìhuàn rénmínbì.

Yíngyèyuán: Hǎo de, qǐng dào nàbian de guìtái tián biǎogé. Zhè shì jīntiān de páijià.

Mǎlì: Jīntiān de duìhuànlǜ hái búcuò.

Yíngyèyuán: Qǐngwèn, nín yào yòng xiànjīn háishi lǚxíng zhīpiào duìhuàn rénmínbì?

Mǎlì: Yòng xiànjīn.

Yíngyèyuán: Yào huàn duōshao qián?

Mǎlì: Liǎngbǎi měiyuán. Nǐmen chúle měiyuán, hái shōu qítā huòbì ma?

Yíngyèyuán: Wǒmen yě shōu yīngbàng、ōuyuán、rìyuán hé gǎngbì、xīntáibì.

Mǎlì: Tài hǎo le. Zěnme bànlǐ shǒuxù?

Yíngyèyuán: Qǐng nín tián yíxià duìhuàn biǎogé.

Mǎlì: Wǒ hái yǒu yìxiē měiyuán xiǎng cún zài yínháng, nǐmen yǒu wàihuì cúnkuǎn ma?

Yíngyèyuán: Yǒu, wǒmen yínháng tígōng quánfāngwèi de fúwù.

二、美元換人民幣

瑪　麗：我想要用美元兑換人民幣。

營業員：好的，請到那邊的櫃檯填表格。這是今天的牌價。

瑪　麗：今天的兑換率還不錯。

營業員：請問，您要用現金還是旅行支票兑換人民幣？

瑪　麗：用現金。

營業員：要換多少錢？

瑪　麗：兩百美元。你們除了美元，還收其他貨幣嗎？

營業員：我們也收英鎊、歐元、日元和港幣、新台幣。

瑪　麗：太好了。怎麼辦理手續？

營業員：請您填一下兑換表格。

瑪　麗：我還有一些美元想存在銀行，你們有外匯存款嗎？

營業員：有，我們銀行提供全方位的服務。

ENGLISH TEXT

Dialogue Ⅱ: Currency Exchange

Mary: I would like to exchange US dollars for *Renminbi.*

Teller: OK. Please go to the counter over there and fill out the form. This is today's exchange rate.

Mary: Today's exchange rate is not bad.

Teller: May I ask if you want to use cash or traveller's checks for the exchange?

Mary: Cash.

Teller: How much would you like to exchange?

Mary: Two hundred US dollars. Do you take other currencies besides US dollars?

Teller: We also take pounds, euros, Japanese yen and Hong Kong dollars, New Taiwanese dollars.

Mary: Great. What do I do to get everything processed?

Teller: Please fill out this money exchange form.

Mary: I also have some US dollars that I would like to deposit in the bank. Do you offer current accounts for foreign currency?

Teller: Yes. Our bank offers complete services.

Notes

Grammar & Pattern Drills

1. 用 (V) "use"

用 is used here in the first part of a serial actions. The phrase of "用＋N" often shows tools，manners or methods of continuous actions.

Subj. ＋用＋N＋V

Examples:

1. 这个美国学生用中文写日记。
   This American student writes his diary in Chinese.
2. 那个美国公司用电子邮件提供服务。
   That American company provides its services by e-mail.

Substitutive drills:

我		电脑	写信。
大卫		信用卡	付钱。
史先生	用	英文	填申报单。
玛丽		外币	兑换人民币。
李小姐		美元	买东西。

2. 还是 (Conj.) "or"

还是 is used to present two or more possibilities in an alternative question. Sometimes，是……还是 can be used as a pair of conjunction words.

Examples:

1. 你是中国人还是日本人?
   Are you Chinese or Japanese?
2. 你喜欢唱歌、看书，还是听音乐?
   Do you like singing, reading, or listening to music?

Substitutive drills:

这是美元	还是	欧元?
你想汇款	还是	贷款?
她是营业员	还是	秘书?
商务中心在楼上	还是	楼下?

3. 除了……(以外)，还…… (Prep..., Adv.) "besides...also"

除了……，还……is often used as a pair to connect two items with the meaning of "in addition to A, there is B". 以外 is optional depending on the length of the structure. If a negative statement follows 除了……（以外），the structure corresponds to "except A, no others".

Examples:

1. 他除了会说汉语（以外），还会说日语。

   Besides Chinese, he can also speak Japanese.

2. 除了提款卡（以外），我还想申请一个信用卡。

   Besides a debit card, I also want to apply for a credit card.

3. 除了美元，我没有别的钱。

   Except for US dollars, I have no other currency.

Substitutive drills:

她		长得漂亮		很聪明。
营业员	除了	说汉语	（以外），还	会说英语。
李小姐		去过法国		去过美国。
大卫来中国		做生意		要学中文。

4. 一下 (Num. + MW) "one time; once"

An action verb attached by 一下 may denote "just do something (for a little while)". It can make the tone of voice moderate and more polite.

Subj. ＋V＋一下＋(Obj.)

Examples:

1. 这是住房登记表，请您填一下。

   This is the check-in form, please fill it out.

2. 你看一下，这是你的照片吗？

Take a look. Is this a picture of you?

Substitutive drills：

我来介绍 她想休息 你坐 请你等	一下。

中国银行金融系统
The Financial & Banking System of China

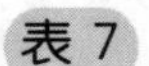

表 7

English	Chinese	*Pinyin*
The People's Bank of China	中国人民银行	Zhōngguó Rénmín Yínháng
Bank of China	中国银行	Zhōngguó Yínháng
Industrial and Commercial Bank of China	中国工商银行	Zhōngguó Gōngshāng Yínháng
Agricultural Bank of China	中国农业银行	Zhōngguó Nóngyè Yínháng
China Construction Bank	中国建设银行	Zhōngguó Jiànshè Yínháng

部分货币的名称
Names of Some Currencies

表 8

English	Chinese	*Pinyin*
US dollar ($)	美元	měiyuán
euro (€)	欧元	ōuyuán
pound sterling (£)	英镑	yīngbàng
Japanese yen (¥)	日元	rìyuán
Singapore dollar (S$)	新加坡元	xīnjiāpōyuán
Australian dollar ($A)	澳元	àoyuán
New Zealand dollar ($NZ)	新西兰元	xīnxīlányuán
rouble (R)	卢布	lúbù
RMB (¥)	人民币	rénmínbì
Hong Kong dollar (HK$)	港币	gǎngbì
New Taiwan dollar (NT$)	新台币	xīntáibì

Day 2: Banking Services

Opening a Bank Account

I'm so proud of myself. Today I opened a bank account——two actually! I opened one for *Renminbi* and one for US dollars because they told me I couldn't deposit and withdraw both currencies in the same account. I had to get some help filling out the paperwork, but it wasn't too hard.

There are no checking accounts in China, only regular passbook savings and certificates of deposit. The interest rates are pretty lousy for regular savings, less than 2% like they are in the USA right now. I found out I can wire money (or have it wired) from the USA to my new account.

Exchange Rates

I exchanged some of my dollars for *Renminbi* at the bank. I could have changed money at my hotel, but their rate was not as good as the bank's. I noticed that the rates for traveller's checks were better than the rates for cash. However, for the best exchange rate, there's always the black market. I didn't know how to find it, but when I came out of the bank, money changers approached me on the street. I didn't change any money with them and later found out from my host that it wasn't safe. I could have ended up with counterfeit bills. China is basically an all cash society, so counterfeit money is everywhere. At the bank and at the shops, I've noticed everyone checking (shaking, holding up to the light, etc.) my cash for authenticity, even US dollars, because of this continuous problem with fakes.

Banking

In China, many different kinds of banking organizations coexist, rationally coordinating the division of responsibility. The People's Bank of China acts as a central bank to exercise macro-control and supervision over the nation's banking business. In 1994, Industrial and Commercial Bank of China, Bank of China, Agricultural Bank of China and China Construction Bank were transformed into national commercial banks. Meanwhile, three policy banks were established: Agricultural Development Bank of China, National Development Bank and China Import and Export Bank. Since 1996, a number of commercial stock banks have been set up. The numbers of financial institutions have increased rapidly, banking businesses have become diversified, and banking services have become an indispensable part of society.

There are some foreign-investment banks established in China too, and some of them have the right to do RMB business. By the end of 2003, a total of 191 commercial foreign financial organizations and 211 agencies of foreign banks had been set up in China.

China's official currency is *Renminbi* (RMB). The basic unit is the *Yuan*. Ten *Jiao* make one *Yuan*, and ten *Fen* make one *Jiao*. Hong Kong's currency is the Hong Kong dollar and Macau's is the Pataca. The exchange rate of RMB is formulated by the People's Bank of China, and issued by the General Administration of Exchange Control. The current exchange rate is 8. 3 *yuan*= US$1. China exercises centralized management over foreign exchange, this function being performed by the General Administration of Exchange Control. At the end of 2004, China's foreign exchange reserves totaled US$609. 9 billion, 258 times that of 1978.

Foreigners holding a tourist visa can open bank accounts in China, including RMB and US dollar accounts, but the latter only at special foreign exchange banks.

第四课 商务会谈
Lesson 4 Business Meeting

Dialogue 1 First Meeting 会面

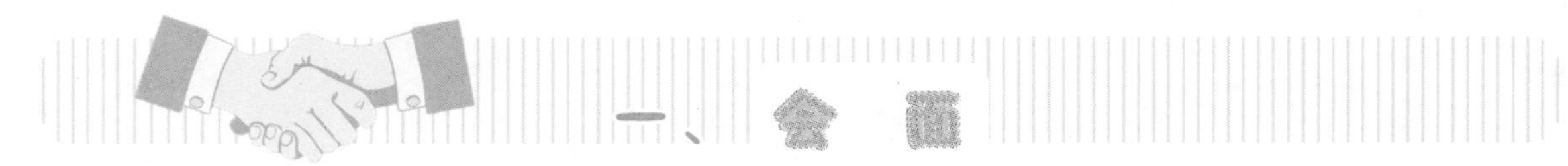

(大卫到达当地公司，预备双方第一次会面。)

经理：欢迎光临本公司！这是我的名片，请多多指教！

大卫：谢谢，这是我的名片。我是美国进出口贸易公司的副总裁，我的中文名字叫史大卫，英文名字叫David Smith。名片上有我的手机号码和电子邮件。

经理：听说您亲自到中国来，我们公司的总裁和董事们都很高兴。现在他们都在会议室等您。会议室在二楼。

大卫：负责出口贸易的主管也来了吗？

经理：来了，分公司的主管都到齐了。

大卫：好极了。对了，开会前让我先把手机关掉。

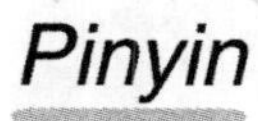

Pinyin

Duìhuà Ⅰ: Huì Miàn

(Dàwèi dàodá dāngdì gōngsī, yùbèi shuāngfāng dì-yī cì huìmiàn.)

Jīnglǐ: Huānyíng guānglín běn gōngsī! Zhè shì wǒ de míngpiàn, qǐng duōduō zhǐjiào!

Dàwèi: Xièxie, zhè shì wǒ de míngpiàn. Wǒ shì Měiguó Jìnchūkǒu Màoyì Gōngsī de fùzǒngcái, wǒ de Zhōngwén míngzi jiào Shǐ Dàwèi, Yīngwén míngzi jiào David Smith. Míngpiàn shang yǒu wǒ de shǒujī hàomǎ hé diànzǐ yóujiàn.

Jīnglǐ: Tīngshuō nín qīnzì dào Zhōngguó lái, wǒmen gōngsī de zǒngcái hé dǒngshìmen dōu hěn gāoxìng. Xiànzài tāmen dōu zài huìyìshì děng nín. Huìyìshì zài èr lóu.

Dàwèi: Fùzé chūkǒu màoyì de zhǔguǎn yě lái le ma?

Jīnglǐ: Lái le, fēn gōngsī de zhǔguǎn dōu dàoqí le.

Dàwèi: Hǎo jí le. Duìle, kāi huì qián ràng wǒ xiān bǎ shǒujī guāndiào.

一、會面

(大衛到達當地公司，預備雙方第一次會面。)

經理：歡迎光臨本公司！這是我的名片，請多多指教！

大衛：謝謝，這是我的名片。我是美國進出口貿易公司的副總裁，我的中文名字叫史大衛，英文名字叫David Smith。名片上有我的手機號碼和電子郵件。

經理：聽說您親自到中國來，我們公司的總裁和董事們都很高興。現在他們都在會議室等您。會議室在二樓。

大衛：負責出口貿易的主管也來了嗎？

經理：來了，分公司的主管都到齊了。

大衛：好極了。對了，開會前讓我先把手機關掉。

ENGLISH TEXT

Dialogue Ⅰ: First Meeting

(David arrived at the local company and prepared for his first meeting.)

Manager: Welcome to our company! Here is my business card for your future reference.

David: Thanks. This is my business card. I am the Vice President of the American Import & Export Trading Company. My Chinese name is Shi Dawei, and my English name is David Smith. My cell phone number and e-mail address are both on the card.

Manager: Our president and board members are happy to see you come to China in person. They are waiting for you in the conference room. The conference room is located on the second floor.

David: Is the person in charge of exports also here?

Manager: Yes. All the supervisors from all the branches are here.

David: Great. By the way, let me turn my cell phone off before our meeting.

Notes

Grammar & Pattern Drills

1. 多多…… (Adv. ＋Adv.) "many; much; more"

多 can be reduplicated before certain verbs in some polite expressions to mean "as much as possible". In general, adjective reduplication will add a vivid effect compared to those without them. Normally, the stress is put on the first adjective, and the reduplicated part is in a neutral tone.

（请）＋多多＋V

Examples:

1. 您年纪大了，多多保重。

   Please take good care of yourself as you are getting older.

2. 我经验不多，请多多指教。

   Please guide me as much as possible, since I don't have much experience.

3. 工作中请多多帮助。

   To do my job, I need as much help as you can give me.

Substitutive drills:

我的中文不好，		指教。
大卫第一次到中国，	请多多	关照。
有招待不周的地方，		包涵。

2. 有 (V) "There is/are (something + somewhere)"

The usage of 有 here is, with place words and/or time words in front, to mean something "exists" at a certain place and/or a certain time. The following NP is the existing "object" that occasionally can be placed before 有.

PW/TW＋有＋NP

Examples:

1. 名片上有我的中文名字和英文名字。
   My Chinese name and my English name are both on my business card.
2. 昨天晚上他家有很多外国客人。
   There were many foreign guests in his home yesterday evening.
3. 这个房间里椅子还有几把，可是桌子没有了。
   There are still several chairs without the table in the room.

Substitutive drills:

北京	有	很多商店。
中国		挺多好玩的地方。
今天晚上		十位外国朋友来。
网吧里		几台手提电脑。

3. 听说 (V) "It was said; hear of"

听说, used as a verb, can be placed in the beginning of a sentence to mean "It was said that". 听说 can also be used as a main verb in a sentence to mean "someone heard that". If someone heard something from a person, that person can be inserted between 听 and 说.

Examples:

1. 听说商务中心的总裁明天要到北京来。
   It is said that the CEO from the Commercial Center will come to Beijing tomorrow.
2. 我听说最近上海发展很快。
   I hear that Shanghai has been developing rapidly recently.
3. 听李小姐说，这个宾馆的服务很好。
   I heard from Miss Li that the service in this hotel is excellent.

Substitutive drills:

听说，
- 很多外国人来中国做生意。
- 北京发展得很快。
- 这家宾馆的服务不好。
- 大卫已经到北京了。

4. VP/clause＋前 (Loc.) "before"

VP/clause＋前 is used as an adverbial phrase to indicate the time before an action or event. 前 sometimes can be replaced by 以前 or 之前.

VP/clause＋前＋main clause

Examples:

1. 您用美元兑换人民币前，请先看看兑换率。
   Please check the exchange rate before you exchange US dollars for *Renminbi*.
2. 申请信用卡以前，要填写申请表格。
   You need to fill out the application form before applying for the credit card.
3. 开会之前，我来介绍一下我们公司的董事。
   Let me introduce the board members in our company before the meeting.

Substitutive drills:

去中国		大卫得办理签证。
过海关	前，	请填好申报单。
到银行开户		李小姐先看了一下定期的利息。

5. 让 (V) "let; allow"

让 here must have an object that also serves as the subject for the following action. The usage of 让 here usually refers to suggestion, causation or allowance.

让＋sb. ＋V

Examples:

1. 您可以让营业员帮您填写这些表格。
   You may ask the clerk to help you fill out these forms.
2. 宾馆让我在我的房间里发电子邮件。
   The hotel allows me to send e-mail in my room.
3. 大卫让玛丽帮他用美元兑换了日元。
   David asked Mary to help him exchange US dollars for Japanese yen.

Substitutive drills:

公司	让	大卫住四星级宾馆。
李小姐		王先生用她的手提电脑。
飞机上不		打手机。
公共场所不		抽烟。

6. 把 (Prep.) " dealing with..."

把 structure in Chinese is also called "the disposal construction" that refers to a verb dealing with both an object and a complement. 把 can be used as a preposition to move the object up before the verb, and leave the complement after the verb.

Subj. ＋把＋Obj. ＋V＋complement or other elements

There are several constraints on the 把 construction.

a. The object that is preposed with 把 always has to be a definite object.

b. The verb has to imply a kind of disposal nature.

c. The verb is always followed by a kind of complement, such as an aspect marker, various complements or verbal constructions.

d. The 把 construction is frequently used with many verbs in Chinese except those verbs with sensory, emotional or existential meanings.

Examples:

1. 请把您的证件给我看一下。
   Please show me your ID.
2. 我把旅行支票兑换成了港币。
   I have exchanged the traveller's check for Hong Kong dollars.

Substitutive drills:

大卫	把	行李	交给了检查人员。
李小姐		大卫	当成朋友。
张先生		申报单	填好了。
服务员		房间钥匙	交给了客人。

公司里的职务与头衔
Positions & Titles in a Company

表 9

English	Chinese	*Pinyin*
CEO	总裁	zǒngcái
CFO	财务主管	cáiwù zhǔguǎn
general manager	总经理	zǒngjīnglǐ
manager	经理	jīnglǐ
chairman of the board of directors	董事长	dǒngshìzhǎng
trustee; board member	董事	dǒngshì
factory director; factory manager	厂长	chǎngzhǎng
sales executive	销售主任	xiāoshòu zhǔrèn
supervisor	主管	zhǔguǎn
marketing executive	市场部主任	shìchǎngbù zhǔrèn

Dialogue 2 Meeting in Progress

开　　会

二、开会

总裁：欢迎，欢迎！一路上辛苦了！哪天到的？

大卫：前天就到了。昨天在北京逛了一下，北京可真大！

经理：请坐，请喝茶。

大卫：谢谢。今天会议的议程是什么？

经理：我们已经准备好了，这是我们的开会内容。

总裁：首先请董事长介绍公司情况，接着请财务主管谈谈合作计划，最后想听听你们的合作意愿。

经理：这是李小姐，由她做翻译。

大卫：有人做会议记录吗？

经理：有，我们有会议记录。会后，秘书会传真一份给您参考。

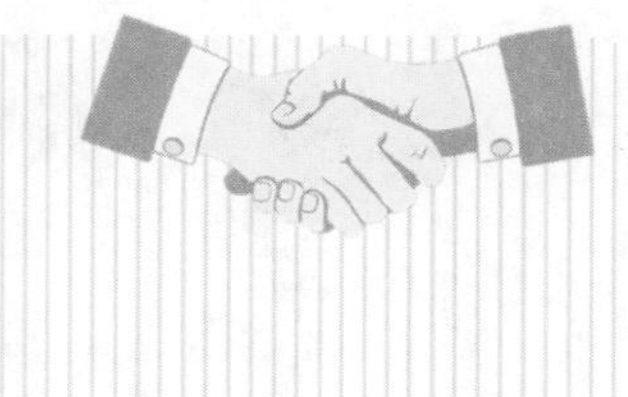

Duìhuà II : Kāi Huì

Zǒngcái: Huānyíng, huānyíng! Yílù shang xīnkǔ le! Nǎ tiān dào de?

Dàwèi: Qiántiān jiù dào le. Zuótiān zài Běijīng guàngle yíxià, Běijīng kě zhēn dà!

Jīnglǐ: Qǐng zuò, qǐng hē chá.

Dàwèi: Xièxie. Jīntiān huìyì de yìchéng shì shénme?

Jīnglǐ: Wǒmen yǐjīng zhǔnbèi hǎo le, zhè shì wǒmen de kāi huì nèiróng.

Zǒngcái: Shǒuxiān qǐng dǒngshìzhǎng jièshào gōngsī qíngkuàng, jiēzhe qǐng cáiwù zhǔguǎn tántan hézuò jìhuà, zuìhòu xiǎng tīngting nǐmen de hézuò yìyuàn.

Jīnglǐ: Zhè shì Lǐ xiǎojie, yóu tā zuò fānyì.

Dàwèi: Yǒu rén zuò huìyì jìlù ma?

Jīnglǐ: Yǒu, wǒmen yǒu huìyì jìlù. Huì hòu, mìshū huì chuánzhēn yí fèn gěi nín cānkǎo.

二、開會

總裁：歡迎，歡迎！一路上辛苦了！哪天到的？

大衛：前天就到了。昨天在北京逛了一下，北京可真大！

經理：請坐，請喝茶。

大衛：謝謝。今天會議的議程是什麽？

經理：我們已經準備好了，這是我們的開會内容。

總裁：首先請董事長介紹公司情况，接着請財務主管談談合作計劃，最後想聽聽你們的合作意願。

經理：這是李小姐，由她做翻譯。

大衛：有人做會議記録嗎？

經理：有，我們有會議記録。會後，秘書會傳真一份給您參考。

ENGLISH TEXT

Dialogue Ⅱ: Meeting in Progress

President: Welcome, welcome! You must be exhausted from your flight here. When did you arrive?

David: The day before yesterday. I walked around Beijing yesterday. Bejing is really a big city!

Manager: Please sit down and have a cup of tea.

David: Thanks. What is the agenda for today's meeting?

Manager: We have prepared the agenda already. This is our meeting outline.

President: First, we would like to ask the chair of the Board to go over our company's overall situation. Then, we will have our staff in charge of finance talk about our collaboration plan. Finally, we would like to hear about your ideas for our partnership.

Manager: This is Miss Li. She will translate for us.

David: Is there anyone keeping the meeting minutes?

Manager: Yes, we keep all our meeting minutes. After the meeting, our secretary will fax you a copy for your reference.

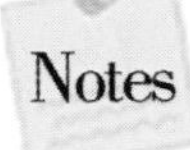

Grammar & Pattern Drills

1. 就 (Adv.) "as early as ..."

就 is used here to emphasize something happened a long time ago. 就 must be placed after time word or other adverbial phrases but before the verb.

Examples:

1. 他从小就想去中国。
   He wanted to go to China ever since his childhood.
2. 总裁上个月就把公司发展计划给董事们了。
   The CEO gave the company's development plan to the board members last month.

Substitutive drills:

大卫	去年		想来中国做生意了。
他	到北京后		给公司发了传真。
李小姐	早上九点	就	到银行去兑换美元了。
我们公司	明天		给你们电汇人民币。
张经理	接到手机短信		打来了电话。

2. ……好了 complement

好了 is used as a complement of the verb to complete the result or condition caused or effected by the action of the verb. Since the action is in a complete stage, there usually is an aspect marker 了 after the complement or at the end of the sentence. In general, the resultative complement can be an adjective or a verb. The negative form always has 没/没有 preceding the verb without 了 at the end of a sentence.

Subj. ＋V＋好了

Examples:

1. 我的申请表已经填好了。
   I have already filled out my application form.
2. 大卫的外汇账户还没有办理好。
   David hasn't opened a foreign currency account yet.
3. 会议的议程准备好了吗?
   Is the agenda for the meeting ready yet?

Substitutive drills:

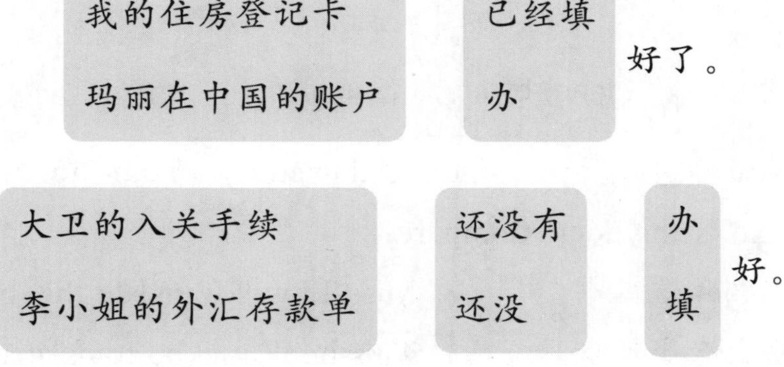

3. 首先……接着……最后…… (Conj.) "firstly...then...finally"

首先……接着……最后 are used here as a group of conjunction words to connect these or more events or actions in order. Note that 首先，接着 or 最后, as conjunction word, can be placed before the subject or at the beginning of each clause which is different from the usage of 先……再……然后……. See Lesson 2-Ⅱ-2.

Example:

大卫首先介绍自己，接着他代表美国公司讲话，最后他和经理们照相。

Firstly, David introduced himself. After that he delivered a speech on behalf of the American company. Finally, he took pictures with the managers.

Substitutive drills:

我们首先	请李总讲话，	接着	请经理介绍，	最后	董事们开会。
	去北京，		到上海，		去美国纽约。
	入关，		去宾馆，		发传真。
	找宾馆，		去银行，		到公司开会。

4. 由 (Prep.) " (done) by sb.; through"

由 here is used as a preposition, followed by a noun, to introduce "someone" who is the doer. Compare:

李小姐要翻译这本书。　Miss Li will translate this book.

这本书要由李小姐翻译。　This book will be translated by Miss Li.

Normally, the "doer" introduced by 由 is pronounced with stress.

Subj. ＋由＋someone＋V

Examples:

1. 我们公司的情况由张经理来介绍。

   Our company's situation will be explained by Manager Zhang.

2. 今天的会议由小李记录。

   The meeting minutes will be taken by Xiao Li .

Substitutive drills:

你的存款手续	由	营业员	办理。
你的健康卡		医生	检查。
大卫的入关申报单		秘书	填写。
今天的会议		李小姐	翻译。

5. ……后 (Loc.) "after; behind"

The usage of 后 is similar to 前. As the antonym of 前, 后 can be used after a noun phrase or a verb phrase to indicate the time with the meaning of "afterwards" or "later". If 后 is used after a place word, it means "behind" the place. The subject of the sentence can be placed either before or after the phrase with 后.

Subj. ＋NP/VP＋后＋VP

Examples:

1. 我晚饭后给李经理发电子邮件。
   I will send Manager Li an e-mail after dinner.
2. 王小姐打完电话后去银行。
   Miss Wang will go to the bank after making a phone call.
3. 会后，公司的董事一起吃晚饭。
   The board members of the company will have dinner together after the meeting.

Substitutive drills:

玛丽	去银行		回宾馆。
大卫	到北京		给你发电子邮件。
我	起床	后	给公司打电话。
张经理	两点半		来开会。
李总裁	开会		去机场。

6. 给 (V/Prep.) "to give; to let"

给 here is used to introduce the doer of the following action, similar to 让, with the meaning of "to let". The object of 给 is actually the "subject" of the following verb.

Subj. ＋给＋sb. ＋VP

Examples:

1. 她买了一本书给我看。

   She bought me a book to read.

2. 营业员给我两张表格填写。

   The clerk gave me two forms and asked me to fill them out.

给 can also be considered as a preposition with the meaning of "for", if the subject is the doer of the main verb.

3. 秘书在北京饭店给张经理订了一个房间。

   The secretary has reserved a room at the Beijing Hotel for Manager Zhang.

Substitutive drills:

张先生	发了一份传真	给	大卫参考。
李小姐	翻译了会议记录		玛丽看。
服务员	拿了一张登记表		王先生填。
董事	准备了一份合作计划		总裁参考。

公司各部门的名称
Names of the Departments in a Company

表 10

English	Chinese	*Pinyin*
headquarters	总公司	zǒnggōngsī
branch office	分公司	fēngōngsī
business office	营业部	yíngyèbù
personnel department	人事部	rénshìbù
human resources department	人力资源部	rénlì zīyuánbù
accounting department	财会部/财务部	cáikuàibù / cáiwùbù
sales department	销售部	xiāoshòubù
international department	国际部	guójìbù
export department	出口部	chūkǒubù
import department	进口部	jìnkǒubù
public relations department	公共关系部	gōnggòng guānxìbù
research & development department	研发部	yánfābù
advertising department	广告部	guǎnggàobù

Day 3: Business Negotiations

Business Meetings

Today we had a formal meeting with our Chinese business partner. Their team consisted of eight people. We only had two. I was surprised to see so many cell phones. My host told me that the telecommunications infrastructure in China is underdeveloped, so cell phones have become popular because they are easier to get than traditional phone lines.

Titles

My co-worker and I exchanged business cards with everyone. I noticed that they looked at our cards and then laid them on the table in front of them. I did the same with their cards, and then my host arranged them. He lined the cards up vertically in front of me with the lowest ranking official on the bottom and the highest on the top. That way I could remember who the important decision makers were. I was glad he did this because I have trouble understanding the titles the Chinese use, such as Director and Vice Director, and knowing which ones are more important than others.

Translators and Meeting Minutes

Our host arranged for Miss Li to be our translator. I think this worked okay, but I wonder whether or not our interests were represented fairly. My co-worker told me later that he thought we should have hired and brought our own translator. I'm trying to get to know our host and build a relationship with him in order to give him a reason to help us in the negotiations. I also asked our host to keep minutes during our meeting. This is not a Chinese custom, so if I hadn't asked, no one would have done it. I also took notes to help me keep track of what was discussed and what was agreed to.

Negotiating

The Chinese are known to be tough negotiators. I'm learning that they don't talk in direct terms or conditions and leave things open for interpretation. They also use questions to express disapproval. I wish I could tell what they are thinking. The Chinese rarely say no, so I have to figure out when their yes means yes, when it means maybe, and when it means no.

Foreign Trade of China

In 2004, China's foreign trade totaled 11. 5 trillion US dollars, increasing by 35. 3% to 2003, ranked 3rd in the world after the US and Germany. Import stood at 5. 6 trillion US dollars, increasing by 36. 6% to 2003, and export stood at 5. 9 trillion US dollars, increasing by 34. 1%. China has become the world's leading consumer in grain, meat, coal, steel, major consumer products and services.

Top Trade Partners of the Mainland of China ($million)

Rank 2004	Country or region	2004	% change	Rank 2003
1	United States	169,626. 20	34. 3	2
2	Japan	167,886. 40	25. 7	1
4	Korea	90,068. 20	42. 5	4
6	Germany	54,124. 30	29. 7	6
7	Singapore	26,683. 90	37. 9	8
8	Malaysia	26,261. 10	30. 5	7
9	Netherlands	21,488. 60	39. 2	10
10	Russia	21,232. 00	34. 7	9
3	Hong Kong	112,678. 40	28. 9	3
5	Taiwan	78,323. 80	34. 2	5

China's Trade with the World ($billion)

	1996	1997	1998	1999	2000	2001	2002	2003	2004
Exports	151. 1	182. 7	184	195	249	266	326	438	593. 4
% change	1. 5	20. 9	0. 5	6. 1	27. 8	6. 8	22. 3	34. 6	35. 4
Imports	138. 8	142. 4	140	166	225	244	295	413	561. 4
% change	5. 1	2. 6	−1. 5	18. 2	35. 8	8. 2	21. 2	39. 9	36
Total	289. 9	325. 1	324	361	474	510	621	851	1,154. 80
% change	3. 2	12. 1	−0. 4	11. 3	31. 5	7. 5	21. 8	37. 1	35. 7

China's Top Imports and Exports in 2004 ($million)

Commodity Description	Imports	Commodity Description	Exports
Electrical machinery & equipment	142,073. 60	Electrical machinery & equipment	129,663. 70
Power generation equipment	91,631. 60	Power generation equipment	118,149. 30
Mineral fuel & oil	48,036. 60	Apparel	54,783. 60
Optical & medical equipment	40,154. 90	Iron & steel	25,216. 40
Iron & steel	28,387. 10	Furniture & bedding	17,318. 60
Plastics & articles thereof	28,060. 10	Optical & medical equipment	16,221. 00
Inorganic & organic chemicals	27,809. 00	Footwear & parts thereof	15,203. 20
Ore, slag & ash	17,292. 70	Toys & games	15,089. 20
Vehicle & parts other than rail	13,102. 70	Mineral fuel & oil	14,475. 70
Copper & articles thereof	10,484. 30	Inorganic & organic chemicals	13,937. 60

第五课 商业宴请
Lesson 5 Business Banquets

Dialogue 1 Hosting Dinner for Visitors 接风

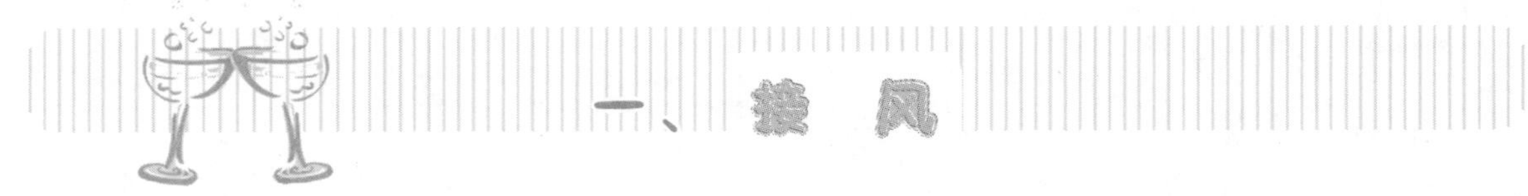

一、接风

大　　卫：谢谢你们特地为我预备的宴席。

业务经理：哪里，哪里！大家请入坐吧！大卫，请坐贵宾席。

大　　卫：谢谢，您也坐吧！

业务经理：给您准备的是西餐餐具，可以吗？

大　　卫：其实，吃中国菜我喜欢用筷子。

业务经理：宴会前，您是否要致辞？

大　　卫：不必了，不必了，我们一边吃一边谈吧。让我举杯祝大家健康！

业务经理：也祝我们的国际贸易合作顺利！

大　　卫：今天的酒菜真丰盛，谢谢主人的热情招待。

业务经理：不用客气，给客人接风是我们中国人的习惯。

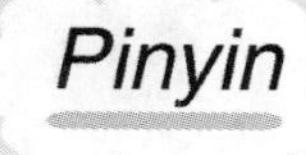

Pinyin

Duìhuà Ⅰ: Jiēfēng

Dàwèi: Xièxie nǐmen tèdì wèi wǒ yùbèi de yànxí。

Yèwù jīnglǐ: Nǎli, nǎli! Dàjiā qǐng rù zuò ba! Dàwèi, qǐng zuò guìbīnxí。

Dàwèi: Xièxie, nín yě zuò ba!

Yèwù jīnglǐ: Gěi nín zhǔnbèi de shì xīcān cānjù, kěyǐ ma?

Dàwèi: Qíshí, chī zhōngguócài wǒ xǐhuan yòng kuàizi。

Yèwù jīnglǐ: Yànhuì qián, nín shìfǒu yào zhì cí?

Dàwèi: Búbì le, búbì le, wǒmen yìbiān chī yìbiān tán ba。 Ràng wǒ jǔ bēi zhù dàjiā jiànkāng!

Yèwù jīnglǐ: Yě zhù wǒmen de guójì màoyì hézuò shùnlì!

Dàwèi: Jīntiān de jiǔcài zhēn fēngshèng, xièxie zhǔren de rèqíng zhāodài。

Yèwù jīnglǐ: Búyòng kèqi, gěi kèren jiēfēng shì wǒmen Zhōngguórén de xíguàn。

一、接風

大　　衛：謝謝你們特地爲我預備的宴席。

業務經理：哪里，哪里！大家請入坐吧！大衛，請坐貴賓席。

大　　衛：謝謝，您也坐吧！

業務經理：給您準備的是西餐餐具，可以嗎？

大　　衛：其實，吃中國菜我喜歡用筷子。

業務經理：宴會前，您是否要致辭？

大　　衛：不必了，不必了，我們一邊吃一邊談吧。讓我舉杯祝大家健康！

業務經理：也祝我們的國際貿易合作順利！

大　　衛：今天的酒菜真豐盛，謝謝主人的熱情招待。

業務經理：不用客氣，給客人接風是我們中國人的習慣。

ENGLISH TEXT

Dialogue Ⅰ: Hosting Dinner for Visitors

David: Thank you for the banquet specifically prepared for me.

Sales manager: You are very welcome! Everybody, please be seated. David, please sit in the distinguished guest seat.

David: Thank you. Please take your seats as well.

Sales manager: I had the waiter bring you Western tableware, is that OK?

David: Well, in fact, I like to use chopsticks when eating Chinese food.

Sales manager: Would you like to give a speech before the banquet?

David: No, no. We can chat with each other while eating. Allow me to give a toast to everyone's health.

Sales manager: I would also like to give a toast to our strong partnership and our international trade.

David: The food and drink are certainly abundant today. Many thanks to the host for your kind hospitality.

Sales manager: You are welcome. It is a Chinese custom to have a dinner of welcome for visitors from afar.

Notes

Grammar & Pattern Drills

1. 为 (Prep.) "for"

为 here is used as a preposition to mean "for" someone or something, and the preposition phrase is always followed by a verb phrase.

Subj. ＋为＋NP＋VP

Examples:

1. 大卫为一家美国公司工作。
   David is working for an American company.
2. 中方经理为美国客人准备了中餐。
   The manager of the Chinese company has prepared Chinese food for the American guests.

为 can also mean "for the purpose of" or "for the sake of". In this case, 而 can be added in between the preposition phrase and the verb/adjectival phrase.

Subj. ＋为＋NP＋而＋VP/AP

3. 我为我们的合作计划而高兴。
   I am glad that we have a cooperation plan.
4. 玛丽为在中国做生意而学习中文。
   Mary is learning Chinese for the sake of doing business in China.

The structure of 为＋NP＋VP sometimes can be used as a modifier followed by 的 to modify a noun phrase.

5. 为我们公司工作的李小姐来了。

   Miss Li who works for our company is coming.

Substitutive drills:

李小姐	为	中美两国的经理	翻译。
大卫		国际贸易公司	工作。
董事们		合作计划	开会。
营业员		外国客人	办理存款手续。

2. 请……吧 "Please...; Would you please...?"

请……吧 can be used as a pair to indicate a suggestion, a request or a mild command in a polite way.

请＋VP＋吧

Examples:

1. 李先生，请谈谈贵公司的计划吧。

   Mr. Li, would you please talk about your company's plan?

2. 王经理，如果你们想进口这些家具，请报价吧。

   Manager Wang, please make an offer if you want to import the furniture.

Substitutive drills:

	上车	
	谈谈	
请	介绍一下	吧。
	把手机关掉	
	准备一下会议议程	

3. "Topic + Comment" Structure

This structure is frequently used in Chinese. The topic of the sentence appears at the beginning of a sentence, and the following comment describes the state, condition or characteristics of the preceding topic. The relationship between the two are similar to superordinate and subordinate or whole and part.

Topic + Comment

Examples:

1. 在中国做生意你得会说中文。

   To do business in China, you have to be able to speak Chinese.

2. 这件美国产品我们觉得不错。

   Regarding this American product, we think it is quite good.

Substitutive drills:

Topic	Comment
在中国住宾馆	需要看个人证件。
在北京入关	要填写申报单。
住宾馆	很方便。
兑换率不错	就多兑换一些人民币。
办理存款账户	有很多手续。
公司的情况	我们请王董事长介绍一下。

4. 一边……，一边…… (Adv.) "at the same time, simultaneously"

一边……，一边…… is used as a pair of adverbs to connect two actions happening at the same time. 一边 is usually placed after the subject and before the verb. The two actions connected by 一边……，一边…… can share the same subject or have two different subjects. 一边……，一边…… can sometimes be simplified as 边……，边…… if two actions share the same subject.

Subj. ＋一边＋VP,（Subj.）＋一边＋VP

Examples:

1. 总裁一边讲话，秘书一边记录。

The secretary is taking notes while the CEO gives a talk.

2. 我一边写电子邮件，一边听音乐。

I am listening to music while writing an e-mail.

3. 玛丽边打电话边发传真。

Mary is talking on the phone while sending a fax.

Substitutive drills:

大卫	一边	填登记表，		一边	跟服务员谈话。
玛丽		看电子邮件，			打电话。
李经理		介绍情况，	史先生		记录。
小张		谈计划，	小王		翻译。

5. 祝 (V) "to wish"

祝 is used as a verb to express good wishes. Normally, there is no need to have a subject unless the subject is not the first person. 祝 can have two objects, but the indirect object can be omitted if it is the second person.

Examples:

1. 祝新年快乐！

I wish you a Happy New Year!

2. 我们公司老板祝贵公司在中国生意好！

Our boss wishes that your business will boom in China.

3. 祝你全家幸福！

I wish that your whole family will be filled with happiness.

Substitutive drills：

	你在北京	生活快乐！
祝	你在美国的生意	成功！
	我们的合作	顺利！

中国商界常用的贺词
Commonly Used Greetings in Chinese Business Circles

表 11

English	Chinese	*Pinyin*
congratulations and may you be prosperous	恭喜发财	gōngxǐ fācái
a small investment brings a ten thousandfold profit	一本万利	yì běn wàn lì
starting business with good luck	开业大吉	kāi yè dà jí
bringing in money or revenue by all possible ways	财源广进	cáiyuán guǎng jìn
rich in financial resources	财源茂盛	cáiyuán màoshèng
the lucky star is in the ascendant	福星高照	fúxīng gāo zhào
the bussiness will be thriving	生意兴隆	shēngyi xīnglóng

星巴克咖啡

KFC

老北京糖葫芦
老北京糖葫芦

Dialogue 2 Expressing Appreciation

答　谢

二、答谢

大　卫：今天我做东答谢你们。你们觉得这家餐厅怎么样？

董事长：有眼光！这家餐厅真不错，有包间，也有宴会厅，还有卡拉OK，很适合开宴会。

大　卫：董事长，请您点菜吧。

董事长：那我就不客气了。

大　卫：我们喝点酒助助兴吧！您喜欢喝葡萄酒还是威士忌？

董事长：我要一杯青岛啤酒，你呢？

大　卫：我倒想尝尝中国的白酒。

董事长：好酒量，小心别醉了！

大　卫：不会的。来，为我们的合作干一杯！

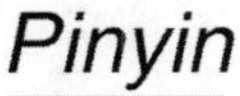

Duìhuà Ⅱ：Dáxiè

Dàwèi： Jīntiān wǒ zuò dōng dáxiè nǐmen. Nǐmen juéde zhè jiā cāntīng zěnmeyàng?

Dǒngshìzhǎng： Yǒu yǎnguāng! Zhè jiā cāntīng zhēn búcuò，yǒu bāojiān，yě yǒu yànhuìtīng，hái yǒu kǎlā-OK，hěn shìhé kāi yànhuì.

Dàwèi： Dǒngshìzhǎng，qǐng nín diǎn cài ba.

Dǒngshìzhǎng： Nà wǒ jiù bú kèqi le.

Dàwèi： Wǒmen hē diǎn jiǔ zhùzhu xìng ba! Nín xǐhuan hē pútaojiǔ háishi wēishìjì?

Dǒngshìzhǎng： Wǒ yào yì bēi Qīngdǎo píjiǔ，nǐ ne?

Dàwèi： Wǒ dào xiǎng chángchang Zhōngguó de báijiǔ.

Dǒngshìzhǎng： Hǎo jiǔliàng，xiǎoxīn bié zuì le!

Dàwèi： Bú huì de. Lái，wèi wǒmen de hézuò gān yì bēi!

二、答謝

大　衛：今天我做東答謝你們。你們覺得這家餐廳怎麼樣？

董事長：有眼光！這家餐廳真不錯，有包間，也有宴會廳，還有卡拉 OK，很適合開宴會。

大　衛：董事長，請您點菜吧。

董事長：那我就不客氣了。

大　衛：我們喝點酒助助興吧！您喜歡喝葡萄酒還是威士忌？

董事長：我要一杯青島啤酒，你呢？

大　衛：我倒想嘗嘗中國的白酒。

董事長：好酒量，小心別醉了！

大　衛：不會的。來，爲我們的合作乾一杯！

ENGLISH TEXT

Dialogue Ⅱ: Expressing Appreciation

David: Today I am hosting a return banquet to extend my appreciation to you. What do you think about this restaurant?

CEO: You made a good choice. This restaurant is really nice. It has separate dinning rooms as well as banquet rooms. It also has Karaoke. It's very good for holding a banquet.

David: Chairman, please go ahead and order.

CEO: OK, then I will help you.

David: Let's drink a bit alcohol to add to the fun. Do you like wine or whisky?

CEO: I would like a glass of Qingdao beer. How about you?

David: I would rather try Chinese liquor.

CEO: You have a good capacity for alcohol. But be careful, don't get drunk!

David: I won't. Come on, let's toast to our future partnership!

Notes

Grammar & Pattern Drills

1. 有……，也有……，还有…… "have A and B, also have C"

有, as a verb, can be used consecutively to list two or more things or activities that are existing or happening. It often represents the whole thing or event by putting every item together.

Topic＋Subj. ＋有 A, 也有 B, 还有 C

Examples:

1. 我的中国朋友中有北京人，也有上海人，还有广州人。
   Among my Chinese friends, some of them are Pekingnese, some are Shanghainese, and some are Cantonese.
2. 今天的晚宴有中餐，也有西餐，饭后还有卡拉 OK。
   We have both Chinese and Western-style foods for dinner tonight. We will also do Karaoke after dinner.
3. 开会的时候，有人讲话，也有人翻译，还有人记录。
   Somebody is speaking, somebody is doing the translation, and somebody is keeping minutes during the meeting.

Substitutive drills:

宴席上	有	啤酒，	也有	葡萄酒，	还有	中国的白酒。
我们公司	有	中国人，	也有	美国人，	还有	日本人。
来开会的	有	公司总裁，	也有	贸易主管，	还有	公司的董事们。
这家商店	有	中国货，	也有	美国货，	还有	日本货。
商业洽谈会上	有	报价的，	也有	还价的，	还有	谈生意的。
商品展示会上	有	批发商，	也有	零售商，	还有	广告商。

2. 适合 (V) "fit, to be suited to"

适合 here is used as a verb to connect one item or one thing to another related one with the meaning of "fit".

A＋(Adv.)＋适合＋B

Examples:

1. 这种手机很适合旅行。

   This type of cell phone is fit for travel.

2. 吃西餐不适合用筷子。

   Chopsticks are not fit for eating Western-style food.

适合 and 合适 have similar meanings. However, 适合 is often used as a verb, whereas 合适 is used as an adjective with the meaning of "suitable".

3. 这些产品的规格很合适。

The specification of these products is suitable.

Substitutive drills:

这些家具	很	适合	这家宾馆。
那些中式服装	不大		美国人。
这类工艺品	非常		美国的市场。
你们的报价	不		买方的要求。

3. 就…… (Adv.) "then; in that case"

就，usually followed by a verb or an adjective phrase，is used to give a conclusion to the preceding meaning or condition. This structure is often ended with 了.

(如果)……,(那)就＋VP/AP＋了

Examples:

1. 如果你们满意，那我们就成交了。

   We will conclude the deal if you are satisfied.

2. 如果你们产品的报价太高，我们就没有利润了。

   We won't make any profit if the price for your products is too high.

Substitutive drills:

你们买方满意，	我们		高兴了。
如果公司请客，	那我		不客气了。
如果兑换率不错，	那我们	就	多换一些人民币。
你们能减价百分之五，	我们		成交了。
要是这些产品的质量没问题，	美国公司		同意进口。

4. 助助兴 "liven things up; add to the fun" *verb reduplication*

助 as a monosyllabic verb, can be reduplicated to add a more vivid or soft effect than those without it. The second repeated syllable is often unstressed and takes a neutral tone.

Subj. ＋V V＋Obj.

Examples:

1. 请你们谈谈美国的名牌货。
   Would you please introduce some of the famous brands of American products?
2. 晚饭后，我们一起唱唱卡拉OK吧。
   Let's sing Karaoke together after dinner.

Substitutive drills:

玛丽想跟李小姐	学学	中文。
王总裁想	听听	董事们的意见。
我们一起来	谈谈	公司的合作计划吧。
小李想帮大卫去跟老板	讨讨	价。
请你们	尝尝	这家餐厅的上海菜。

5. 倒…… (Adv.) "unexpectedly"

倒, as an adverb, is used before the verb phrase to indicate something unexpected in a certain context.

Subj. ＋倒＋VP

Examples:

1. 玛丽是美国人，可她倒喜欢喝中国茶。
   Mary is an American, but she likes to drink Chinese tea.
2. 这件中式衣服很漂亮，价钱倒不贵。
   This Chinese style dress is very pretty. Surprisingly, it is very inexpensive.

Substitutive drills:

北京人很多，	买东西	倒	很方便。
这件工艺品的报价很高，	玛丽		觉得很合理。
这是美国的名牌货，	李先生		看不上。
大卫是美国人，	吃饭时		喜欢用筷子。

6. 小心 (V/Adj.) "be cautious; careful"

小心 can be used either as a verb or an adjective depending on the context. It can be followed by an object when it is used as a verb, and the object can be a noun phrase, a verb phrase or a clause. Normally, it doesn't need to have a subject in an imperative sentence.

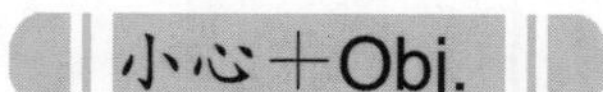

小心＋Obj.

Examples:

1. 小心轻放！

   Handle with care!

2. 旅行的时候，小心你的护照和贵重物品。

   Be careful with your passport and valuable things when you are traveling.

小心 can also be used as an adjective.

Subj. ＋ (Adv.) ＋小心

Example:

3. 她在银行兑换外币的时候很小心。

   She was very careful when she exchanged foreign money at the bank.

Substitutive drills:

A. 小心 as a verb:

中国的白酒跟啤酒不一样，	小心	别喝多了。
旅行的时候		你的钱。
出国以后		带好护照。

B. 小心 as an adjective:

玛丽入关的时候	很	小心。
大卫存放贵重物品时	不大	
中方公司报价的时候	非常	

中国的四大菜系
The Four Major Systems of Chinese Cuisine

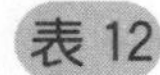
表 12

English	Chinese	*Pinyin*
Shandong cuisine	鲁菜/山东菜	lǔcài / Shāndōngcài
Cantonese cuisine	粤菜/广东菜	yuècài / Guǎngdōngcài
Sichuan cuisine	川菜/四川菜	chuāncài / Sìchuāncài
Huaiyang cuisine	淮扬菜	huáiyángcài

Day 4: Business Banquet

Food Culture

The Chinese love to eat! This evening, I attended my second banquet and it was as thrilling, exasperating, and LONG as the first.

Once again, I was surprised by how the alcohol flowed. All the men drank beer with the meal, but it was heavily supplemented by rice whisky (*baijiu*). A toast was made with each shot of *baijiu*, and, as the guest, I was expected to make a toast as well. I simply said that I appreciated the warm welcome I received and hoped my new Chinese friends would visit me in America. Interestingly, the women at the banquet did not drink beer, but some of them drank *baijiu* during the toasts. The Chinese know alcohol reduces inhibitions and believe it reveals one's true character and personality. They want to be sure they can trust anyone with whom they do business. My host told me the only polite way to refuse alcohol is to say you have a bad stomach and can't drink for health reasons. He said if a person can drink, but simply doesn't like the taste, he'll have a hard time convincing his Chinese counterparts that he is open, honest, friendly and interested in forming a lasting business relationship.

At times, during the meal, it seemed like everyone was drinking and no one was eating. However, since the banquet lasted close to three hours, there was plenty of time to eat later. The food just kept coming during the first two hours, so I shouldn't have eaten so much at the beginning. I can't use chopsticks very well, so my host helped me by putting food on my plate. This made me feel like a child, but I found out later it was honoring. I wanted to try some of every dish, but some looked bad and tasted even worse, so I simply couldn't eat it. I kept struggling with my chopsticks and finally asked the waitress for a knife and fork. Everyone laughed and no one seemed offended.

The banquet was held in a private room around a large, round table with a Lazy Susan in the middle. I noticed that the seating arrangement was very important. Luckily, I didn't sit down at the table until I was shown which seat was mine. We all sat on couches nearby and chatted and drank tea until all the guests arrived. My host told me that the person who sits directly across from the doorway is usually the most important. The persons to his right and left are the honored guests (me!). The person who sits with his back to the doorway (directly across from the most important person) is usually the host. This person usually pôurs drinks for everyone, deals with the wait staff and pays the bill.

I also learned that if a Chinese person invites me to dinner, he will pay for my meal. Furthermore, my host told me if I eat with a group of American friends while in China, it is not polite for each person to take out his money and split the bill in front of the waitress, even though this is acceptable in America. The best thing to do is to let one person pay the bill and then settle with the others later.

Banquets

Chinese cuisine is an important part of Chinese culture. It is unique and famous all over the world. France, Turkey and Chinese foods are called the "three famous cuisine systems" in the world. Through the years, four major systems of cooking have taken shape: Shandongnese, Huaiyangnese, Sichuanese and Guangdongnese. Each of them are comprised of thousands of different famous foods. Altogether, there are more than ten thousand specialty dishes.

On all streets there are numerous restaurants, some of them have a long gastronomic histories and are famous all over the world. These include the *Donglaishun* (东来顺) restaurant, the *Quanjude* (全聚德) restaurant in Beijing; the *Songhelou* (松鹤楼) Restaurant in Suzhou; and the *Laozhenxing* (老振兴) Restaurant in Shanghai. Nowdays there are more and more Western restaurants in China, such as McDonald's, Pizza Hut, and Kentucky Fried Chicken. Most star-rated hotels have a Western restaurant. They are becoming more and more popular in China.

In China, restaurants are usually used for friends and business partners to celebrate holidays and success, so it's normal for Chinese companies to treat their partners to dinner or banquets. During business banquets, people are often dressed in suits to show their appreciation and respect to the hosts, and the hosts usually illustrate their hospitality by ordering abundant quantities of food for their guests. Additionally, due to a long history of wine culture, drinking various types of wine like rice wine is common during a business banquet.

CAROL & JOHN'S
JOY & Peace
OMEGA
OMEGA

第六课 洽谈生意
Lesson 6 Business Discussions

Dialogue 1 Price Negotiation | 议价

一、议价

大卫：下星期的商业洽谈会，你准备好了吗？

玛丽：差不多了。这是中方出口公司的报价单。

大卫：看起来，家具和服装的价格比较合理，规格大小也合适。

玛丽：是呀，这些产品的质量也没有问题，又便宜又好。进口到美国以后，一定畅销。

大卫：但愿这样。不过，我觉得工艺品的报价有点儿高。其中，项链、耳环的款式也不太符合我们美国人的眼光。

玛丽：可不是嘛！不中不西的，我也看不上。反正我们可以讨价还价。价钱低的话，我们可以先试销。

大卫：好，看你的。如果投资回报率高，我会给你红利的。

玛丽：谢谢“大”老板！

Pinyin

Duìhuà Ⅰ：Yì Jià

Dàwèi：Xià xīngqī de shāngyè qiàtánhuì，nǐ zhǔnbèi hǎo le ma?

Mǎlì：Chàbuduō le. Zhè shì Zhōngfāng chūkǒu gōngsī de bàojiàdān.

Dàwèi：Kàn qilai，jiājù hé fúzhuāng de jiàgé bǐjiào hélǐ，guīgé dàxiǎo yě héshì.

Mǎlì：Shì ya，zhè xiē chǎnpǐn de zhìliàng yě méiyǒu wèntí，yòu piányi yòu hǎo. Jìnkǒu dào Měiguó yǐhòu，yídìng chàngxiāo.

Dàwèi：Dànyuàn zhèyàng. Búguò，wǒ juéde gōngyìpǐn de bàojià yǒudiǎnr gāo. Qízhōng，xiàngliàn、ěrhuán de kuǎnshì yě bú tài fúhé wǒmen Měiguórén de yǎnguāng.

Mǎlì：Kěbushì ma! Bù Zhōng bù Xī de，wǒ yě kàn bu shàng. Fǎnzhèng wǒmen kěyǐ tǎo jià huán jià. Jiàqián dī dehuà，wǒmen kěyǐ xiān shìxiāo.

Dàwèi：Hǎo，kàn nǐ de. Rúguǒ tóuzī huíbàolǜ gāo，wǒ huì gěi nǐ hónglì de.

Mǎlì：Xièxie “dà” lǎobǎn!

一、議價

大衛：下星期的商業洽談會，你準備好了嗎？

瑪麗：差不多了。這是中方出口公司的報價單。

大衛：看起來，傢俱和服裝的價格比較合理，規格大小也合適。

瑪麗：是呀，這些產品的質量也沒有問題，又便宜又好。進口到美國以後，一定暢銷。

大衛：但願這樣。不過，我覺得工藝品的報價有點兒高。其中，項鏈、耳環的款式也不太符合我們美國人的眼光。

瑪麗：可不是嘛！不中不西的，我也看不上。反正我們可以討價還價。價錢低的話，我們可以先試銷。

大衛：好，看你的。如果投資回報率高，我會給你紅利的。

瑪麗：謝謝“大”老闆！

ENGLISH TEXT

Dialogue Ⅰ: Price Negotiation

David: Are you ready for the business meeting next week?

Mary: Almost. Here is the price list from the Chinese Export Company.

David: The price for furniture and clothing seems reasonable. The specification and size meet our requirements as well.

Mary: Yes, there is no problem with the quality of these products. The products are good and inexpensive. They will be in great demand when imported to the USA.

David: I hope so. However, I think the prices of handicrafts are a bit high. Also, the design of the necklaces and earrings may not meet the tastes of our people.

Mary: That is right. These are neither Chinese nor Western. They are not my style. Well, we can always bargain for them. If the price is not too high, we can put them on the test market.

David: OK, we are counting on you. If we get a high return, I will share the bonus with you.

Mary: Thank you, "big" boss!

Notes

Grammar & Pattern Drills

1. 下(个)星期 (TW) "next week"

Other common time expressions are:

Day and Year

大前天	前天	昨天	今天	明天	后天	大后天
大前年	前年	去年	今年	明年	后年	大后年

Month and Week

上上个月	上个月	这个月	下个月	下下个月
上上个星期	上个星期	这个星期	下个星期	下下个星期

Note：前 and 上，后 and 下 cannot be interchanged.

2. 看起来 (Interj.) "it seems；appears"

看起来 can be used as a fixed phrase to interject into a sentence with the meaning of "it looks like" or "by estimate". However，V＋起来 implies that an action or state has just started. 了 can be placed between the verb and 起来 or after.

Subj. ＋V＋起来＋了

Subj. ＋V＋了＋起来

Examples:

1. 他笑起来了。

   He's started laughing.

2. 经理们谈了起来。

   The managers have started to chat.

When an object follows the verb, it is placed between 起 and 来.

Subj. ＋V＋起＋Obj. ＋来（了）

Examples:

1. 妹妹唱起歌来了。

   Little sister has started to sing.

2. 李先生在美国做起生意来了。

   Mr. Li has started to do business in the USA.

Substitutive drills:

到中国后，大卫	忙了起来。
李总裁跟王小姐	跳起舞来。
他到公司后	就打起电话来。
我用电脑	写起电子邮件来。

3. 比较 (Adv.) "fairly; comparatively"

The original meaning of 比较 is to compare. However, 比较 means "relatively" or "comparatively" if it is used as an adverb. You can think of it this way:

A is better than B. ⟹ A is better comparatively.

A 比 B 好。⟹ A 比较好。

Example:

我爸爸比我高。⟹我爸爸比较高。

My father is taller than me. ⟹ My father is quite tall.

Substitutive drills:

定期的利率比活期高。	⟹	定期的利率比较高。
信用卡比支票方便。		信用卡比较方便。
今天比昨天热。		今天比较热。

4. 又……又…… (Adv. ...Adv. ...) "both... and..."

It is a set of correlative markers that connect two similar items or descriptions.

Examples:

1. 这家商店的东西又好又便宜。

   The goods sold in this store are both good and inexpensive.

2. 小王又会说中文又会说英文。

   Xiao Wang can speak both Chinese and English.

Substitutive drills:

弟弟长得		高		胖。
那个学生	又	聪明	又	用功。
这个电影		紧张		有意思。
妈妈		做饭		洗衣服。

5. 不A不B (Adv. ...Adv. ...) "neither...nor..."

不 A 不 B is a commonly used expression in Chinese which could have different indications depending on the meanings of A and B.

(1) If A and B are monosyllabic verbs which are similar in meaning, 不 A 不 B is an emphatic negative form.

不吃不喝　　don't eat anything at all

不闻不问　　not bother to ask or to listen

(2) If A and B are opposite in meaning, 不 A 不 B means:

a. just right (positive)

不大不小　（neither big nor small）just fit

b. neither... nor... (negative)

不中不西 (neither Chinese nor Western) not a right style

不上不下 (neither up nor down) be suspended in mid air

(3) If A and B are related in meaning, A is the cause, B shows the result.

不看不行 (If not..., then not...)

It won't be all right unless you take a look.

Substitutive drills:

这件衣服	不	大	不	小	，	很合适。
这种款式	不	中	不	西	，	没有人喜欢。
他们的产品	不	好	不	坏	，	马马虎虎。
我们	不	减价	不	行	，	打不开销路。

有关价格的常用词语
Common Expressions on Price

表 13

English	Chinese	*Pinyin*
rise in price	涨价/提价	zhǎng jià / tí jià
reduction in price	减价/降价	jiǎn jià / jiàng jià
(commodity) price	物价	wùjià
high-priced	高价	gāojià
low-priced	廉价	liánjià
special offer	特价	tèjià
negotiate a price	议价	yì jià
stabilize prices	平价	píngjià
appraised price	估价	gūjià
quoted price	报价	bàojià
counter-offer	还价	huán jià
bargain	讨价还价	tǎo jià huán jià
inexpensive but elegant	价廉物美	jià lián wù měi
price index	价格指数	jiàgé zhǐshù
price subsidies	价格补贴	jiàgé bǔtiē
price list	价目表	jiàmùbiǎo
preferential price	优惠价	yōuhuìjià

北京市百货大楼

Dialogue 2 Closing the Deal

成　　交

二、成交

王经理：玛丽小姐，我们给贵公司的商品目录和报价单，你们满意吗？

大　卫：关于家具和服装，我们比较满意。但是，贵公司是否可以再考虑一下工艺品的报价？

玛　丽：作为进出口批发商，我们要先印广告、开商品展示会，再通过销售网，在全国试销。如果价格高，恐怕打不开销路。

张小姐：可是，请看这些商品的商标，都是中国的名牌。

玛　丽：不知贵方是否考虑到我们还要付关税，加上零售商的回扣，我们公司的利润就太低了。

王经理：作为卖方，我们应该尽量满足买方的要求。如果我们减价百分之十，贵方觉得怎么样？

大　卫：那太好了！我们成交了！

王经理：一言为定！

Duìhuà II: Chéng Jiāo

Wáng jīnglǐ: Mǎlì xiǎojie, wǒmen gěi guì gōngsī de shāngpǐn mùlù hé bàojiàdān, nǐmen mǎnyì ma?

Dàwèi: Guānyú jiājù hé fúzhuāng, wǒmen bǐjiào mǎnyì. Dànshì, guì gōngsī shìfǒu kěyǐ zài kǎolǜ yíxià gōngyìpǐn de bàojià?

Mǎlì: Zuòwéi jìn-chūkǒu pīfāshāng, wǒmen yào xiān yìn guǎnggào、kāi shāngpǐn zhǎnshìhuì, zài tōngguò xiāoshòuwǎng, zài quán guó shìxiāo. Rúguǒ jiàgé gāo, kǒngpà dǎ bu kāi xiāolù.

Zhāng xiǎojie: Kěshì, qǐng kàn zhèxiē shāngpǐn de shāngbiāo, dōu shì Zhōngguó de míngpái.

Mǎlì: Bù zhī guìfāng shìfǒu kǎolǜ dào wǒmen hái yào fù guānshuì, jiā shang língshòushāng de huíkòu, wǒmen gōngsī de lìrùn jiù tài dī le.

Wáng jīnglǐ: Zuòwèi màifāng, wǒmen yīnggāi jǐnliàng mǎnzú mǎifāng de yāoqiú. Rúguǒ wǒmen jiǎn jià bǎi fēn zhī shí, guìfāng juéde zěnmeyàng?

Dàwèi: Nà tài hǎo le! Wǒmen chéng jiāo le!

Wáng jīnglǐ: Yì yán wèi dìng!

二、成交

王經理：瑪麗小姐，我們給貴公司的商品目録和報價單，你們滿意嗎？

大　衛：關於傢俱和服裝，我們比較滿意。但是，貴公司是否可以再考慮一下工藝品的報價？

瑪　麗：作爲進出口批發商，我們要先印廣告、開商品展示會，再通過銷售網，在全國試銷。如果價格高，恐怕打不開銷路。

張小姐：可是，請看這些商品的商標，都是中國的名牌。

瑪　麗：不知貴方是否考慮到我們還要付關稅，加上零售商的回扣，我們公司的利潤就太低了。

王經理：作爲賣方，我們應該盡量滿足買方的要求。如果我們減價百分之十，貴方覺得怎麽樣？

大　衛：那太好了！我們成交了！

王經理：一言爲定！

ENGLISH TEXT

Dialogue Ⅱ: Closing the Deal

Manager Wang: Mary, are you OK with the product catalogue and price list we gave you?

David: In terms of furniture and clothing, we are satisfied. However, can your company rethink the offering price for handicrafts?

Mary: As the export and import wholesaler, we have to print advertisements, display merchandise, and put products in national test markets through distribution networks. If the price is too high, I am afraid we won't be able to sell enough.

Miss Zhang: But look at the labels on these products. They are famous brands in China.

Mary: I wonder if your company knows we still have to pay duty along with a sales commission. We will barely make any profit.

Manager Wang: As the seller, we should meet the buyer's needs as much as possible. How about we reduce the price by 10%?

David: That is great. Done deal!

Manager Wang: Then it's settled.

Grammar & Pattern Drills

1. 关于 (Prep.) "about; with regard to"

关于 is used as a preposition that introduces the scope of an activity or subject. With the sense of "about" or "concerning", it can be used in two ways:

(1) It is used to make an adverbial modifier.

Examples:

1. 关于他的事情，我不想再听了。
   I don't want to hear about him and his situation any more.
2. 关于中国经济，她知道得很多。
   She knows a lot about the Chinese economy.

(2) It is used to make a prepositional phrase modifying the object of a sentence. The particle 的 is placed before the object it modifies.

3. 老师说了一个关于中国的故事。
   The teacher told a story about China.
4. 这是一本关于旅行的书。
   This is a book about travelling.

Substitutive drills:

关于	服装的款式，	请你们考虑一下。
	贵方的报价，	我们很满意。

大卫想谈谈	关于	中国商品	的	商标。
王经理介绍了		销售网		问题。

2. 是否 (Adv.) "whether or not; whether"

是否 is usually used in written Chinese. 是否 and 是不是 are similar in meaning. However, 是不是 can be followed by a noun or a pronoun, e. g. 是不是你，but 是否 can't，是否你 is wrong.

Examples:

1. 你是否可以借我这本书？⟹你是不是可以借我这本书？
   Could you lend me this book?
2. 你是否喜欢唱歌？⟹你是不是喜欢唱歌？
   Do you like singing?

Substitutive drills:

你	是否	考虑了关税的问题？
玛丽		知道买方的要求？
这种商品		会减价？

3. 作为 (Prep.) "in the capacity of; as"

作为 can be followed by a noun or noun phrase, used at the beginning of the sentence to form a prepositional phrase.

Examples:

1. 作为出口商，他知道外国人喜欢什么。

   As an exporter, he knows what foreigners like.

2. 作为经理，应该考虑员工的要求。

   As the manager, you should consider the employee's needs.

Substitutive drills:

作为	零售商，	他常常拿到回扣。
	老板，	大卫要给员工红利。
	进口商，	一定要有销售网。
	买方，	我们觉得商品的价格太高。

4. 恐怕 (Adv.) "perhaps; I am afraid..."

恐怕, an adverb, is usually used in a negative prediction, and it carries the mild sense of "afraid". Therefore, 恐怕 is different from 怕 (fear), which is a verb. The subject of 恐怕 is always understood as "I", no matter "I" appears or not in a sentence.

Examples:

1. 天这么黑，恐怕要下雨了。

   The sky is getting darker, I am afraid it's going to rain.

2. 已经很晚了，他恐怕不会来了。

   It's already very late, I am afraid that he will not come.

Substitutive drills:

家具的质量	恐怕	不太好。
零售商的回扣		太高了。
他们的要求		不能满足。

5. 打不开 (V+complement) "can't open"

"V+得/不+complement" is the form of potential complement. If you wish to express an action's potential result which may or may not be accomplished by one's capability, you may simply insert 得 with the sense of "be able to" between the first verb and the complement to indicate a positive potential, or insert 不 to indicate a negative potential result. So, 得 and 不 are the markers of a potential complement, and a positive form with a negative form can make a question, such as 打得开打不开?

Substitutive drills:

大卫	听	得	懂中文。
这些进口商品一定	打		开销路。
张小姐	买		起这件工艺品。

玛丽恐怕看	不	懂中文。
这种项链卖		出去。
在这个商店买		到名牌货。

有关"税"的常用词语
Common Expressions on Tax

表 14

English	Chinese	*Pinyin*
customs duty; tariff	关税	guānshuì
income tax	所得税	suǒdéshuì
evade tax	偷税	tōu shuì
tax evasion	漏税	lòu shuì
tax bureau	税务局	shuìwùjú
collect tax	收税	shōu shuì
tax rate	税率	shuìlǜ
tax revenue	税收	shuìshōu
tax collector	税务员	shuìwùyuán
taxation	税款	shuìkuǎn
pay tax	上/缴/纳税	shàng/jiǎo/nà shuì
exemption from customs duties	关税豁免	guānshuì huòmiǎn
tariff preference	关税优惠	guānshuì yōuhuì
reduce tax	减税	jiǎn shuì

Day 5: Responding to an Offer and Booking an Order

Bargaining vs. Negotiating

Last night I went out to do some shopping. I saw a street vendor selling fruit and decided to buy some for my host. Fruit is always a good gift, especially if you're visiting a Chinese family. Fruit is sold by weight, usually 500 grams (or half a kilogram), which is one *jin*. Vendors quote prices per *jin*. I wanted four *jin* of bananas (*xiangjiao*) and was quoted 4. 5 *kuai* per *jin*. I talked the vendor down to 3 *kuai* per *jin* and struck a bargain. It seemed easy and I was proud of myself until I got back to the hotel. I showed my purchase to one of the girls at the front desk and she told me I paid too much! She would have gotten the same bananas for 1. 5 to 2 *kuai* per *jin*! She told me a good rule of thumb for bargaining is to wait until the vendor quotes a price, then take 40% of it and make that your offer. The vendor will probably frown, but come back with a counter offer. Then you can make another offer, slowly moving up towards 50% of the original asking price. You should never pay more than 50% of the asking price unless you really want an item. The process of bargaining back and forth is what the Chinese enjoy so much and many foreigners get hooked as well. The bad news is this form of bargaining doesn't work in the boardroom.

Business negotiations take more time and involve many

more details, such as who pays shipping, insurance and taxes. Each of these details must be discussed. I'm learning that the Chinese like win-win solutions as much as Americans, but they also expect some concessions and compromise. They want to establish a friendship first and a business relationship second. Once an agreement is reached, that is only the beginning of a relationship that needs continued nurturing. If no effort is put into the relationship after a contract is signed, the Chinese will be unhappy and probably not honor the contract.

Brand Names and Sales Network

While I was out shopping, I noticed bicycles for sale in a department store. A sales clerk told me that brand name is important to Chinese shoppers. The two most famous brands of bicycles in China are Forever and Phoenix. China has a vast sales network, including many street markets and street vendors. However, the highest quality foreign-made products are always sold in department stores. Most American products are very desirable in China.

Speaking of bicycles, they are still the number one form of transportation in China and they are everywhere! Outside every department store is a sea of bicycles parked side by side. Since bikes are often stolen, an attendant usually watches them (for a small fee paid when you leave) while the owners are inside shopping. When a strong wind blows, all the bicycles go tumbling down like dominos! After seeing that, I have a new business idea——stronger locks and kickstands for bicycles!

China's Foreign Investment

China, since the economic restructuring in 1978, has been the greatest recipient of foreign directed investment (FDI) among developing countries, and it's the second-largest recipient of FDI in the world after the United States. In 2004, the FDI totaled $153. 5 billion, up almost 34 percent than 2003, and the total utilized FDI was $60. 63 billion by the end of 2004, up 13. 3 percent.

FDI by Investment Vehicle in China, 2004

	Number of Contracts			Amount Contracted			Amount Utilized		
		% change	% of total	$ billion	% change	% of total	$ billion	% change	% of total
Foreign Direct Investment (FDI)	43,664	6. 29	100	153. 47	33. 38	100	60. 63	13. 32	100
Equity Joint Ventures	11,570	−7. 6	26. 5	27. 64	8. 37	18	16. 39	6. 46	27
Contractual Joint Ventures	1,343	−13. 19	3. 08	7. 79	4. 13	5. 08	3. 11	−18. 88	5. 12
Wholly Foreign-Owned Enterprises	30,708	13. 97	70. 3	117. 28	43. 7	76. 4	40. 22	20. 49	66. 3
Shareholding Ventures	37	94. 74	0. 09	0. 39	−47. 37	0. 34	0. 33	−52. 93	0. 62
Joint Resource Exploration	8	100	0. 02	0. 09	57. 09	0. 08	0. 03	−87. 71	0. 06

Utilized FDI in China ($ billion), 1980~2004

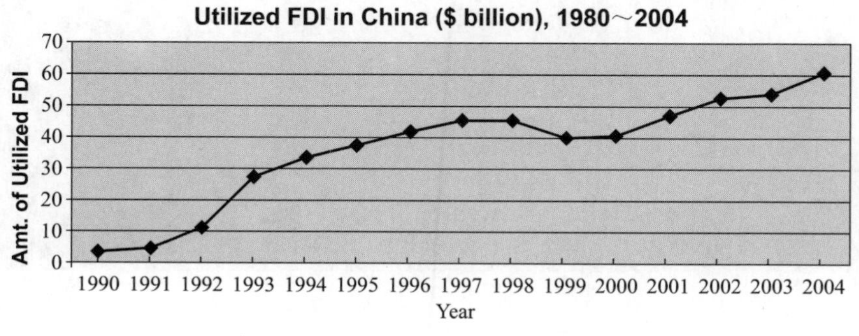

北京市图书进出口

Appendices 附录

Appendix 1：Map of China

Major Cities：

1. 北京	Běijīng	5. 台北	Táiběi	(Taipei)
2. 上海	Shànghǎi	6. 香港	Xiānggǎng	(Hong Kong)
3. 天津	Tiānjīn	7. 澳门	Àomén	(Macau)

4. 重庆　Chóngqìng

Appendix 2：Special Administration Regions

1. 香港特别行政区　Xiānggǎng Tèbié Xíngzhèngqū
   Hong Kong Special Administrative Region
2. 澳门特别行政区　Àomén Tèbié Xíngzhèngqū
   Macau Special Administrative Region

Appendix 3：Special Economic Zones

经济特区	Jīngjì Tèqū	Special Economic Zones	
1. 深圳	Shēnzhèn	(in Guangdong Province)	1980
2. 珠海	Zhūhǎi	(in Guangdong Province)	1980
3. 汕头	Shàntóu	(in Guangdong Province)	1980
4. 厦门	Xiàmén	(in Fujian Province)	1980
5. 海南	Hǎinán	(Hainan Province)	1988

Appendix 4：Coastal Cities Open to Foreign Investment

沿海开放城市	Yánhǎi Kāifàng Chéngshì	Coastal Cities Open to Foreign Investment	1984
(由北至南)	(yóu běi zhì nán)	(from North to South)	
1. 大连	Dàlián	(in Liaoning Province)	
2. 秦皇岛	Qínhuángdǎo	(in Hebei Province)	
3. 天津	Tiānjīn	(a municipality directly under the Central Government)	

4. 烟台	Yāntái	(in Shandong Province)
5. 青岛	Qīngdǎo	(in Shandong Province)
6. 连云港	Liányúngǎng	(in Jiangsu Province)
7. 南通	Nántōng	(in Jiangsu Province)
8. 上海	Shànghǎi	(a municipality directly under the Central Government)
9. 宁波	Níngbō	(in Zhejiang Province)
10. 温州	Wēnzhōu	(in Zhejiang Province)
11. 福州	Fúzhōu	(in Fujian Province)
12. 广州	Guǎngzhōu	(in Guangdong Province)
13. 湛江	Zhànjiāng	(in Guangdong Province)
14. 北海	Běihǎi	(in Guangxi Autonomous Region)

Appendix 5：Coastal Economic Development Zones

沿海经济开放区	Yánhǎi Jīngjì Kāifàngqū	Coastal Economic Development Zones	
1. 长江三角洲	Cháng Jiāng Sānjiǎozhōu	Yangtze River Delta	1995
2. 珠江三角洲	Zhū Jiāng Sānjiǎozhōu	Pearl River Delta	1995
3. 厦漳泉三角洲	Xià-Zhāng-Quán Sānjiǎozhōu	Xiamen-Zhangzhou-Quanzhou Area in Southern Fujian Province	1995

Acknowledgements

This business Chinese textbook series is one of the teaching material projects supported by the Chinese National Office for Teaching Chinese as a Foreign Language (NOTCFL). The office has been very encouraging in the implementation of this project we have undertaken. Our special thanks are due to Mr. Song Yongbo and Mr. Zhang Tonghui from the Department of Teaching and Research of NOTCFL for their guidance and assistance. We are also very grateful to the editors of Beijing Language and Culture University Press for their valuable suggestions.

The chief editor of the textbook series is Dr. Xiaojun Wang, associated with Professor Zhang Wangxi and Professor Sun Dejin. Dr. Joy Huang, Ms. Linda Kuo and Ms. Cammy Chen made great contributions to the contents and exercises of this textbook series. Mr. David Silvey largely wrote the business and cultural notes while Ms. Yin Huiying, who also helped with the typing, provided most of the economic information. Mr. Alexander Donovan thoroughly proofread the English texts.

As teachers, we owe tremendous thanks to our students. We also owe our heartfelt thanks to our colleagues, especially to Dr. Timothy Light who kindly read the textbook and wrote the preface, to Dr. Cynthia Running-Johnson, and to numerous other colleagues for their inspirations.

The Authors

鸣 谢

本教材为中国国家对外汉语教学领导小组办公室规划教材。汉办对这一项目非常支持，教学处宋永波先生、张彤辉先生一直给予具体指导与协助。北京语言大学出版社的编辑为本教材提出了很好的修改意见，特此一并致谢。

本教材由王晓钧教授负责具体的编写工作，由张旺熹教授、孙德金教授共同策划审定。Joy Huang 博士、Linda Kuo Rice 女士和 Cammy Chen 女士协助编写课文和练习，David Silvey 先生主要撰写商业文化的比较，尹惠莹女士提供经贸信息部分并负责初稿的打字输入，Alexander Donovan 先生校读了全书的英文部分。

作为教师，我们要特别感谢我们的学生。我们也要衷心感谢黎天睦教授拨冗阅读全稿并为本教材作序，同时感谢 Cynthia Running-Johnson 博士等诸多同事的鼓励。

编者